CALLED *to be*
GOD'S LEADER
WORKBOOK

CALLED *to be* GOD'S LEADER WORKBOOK

HOW GOD PREPARES HIS SERVANTS *for* SPIRITUAL LEADERSHIP

HENRY BLACKABY & RICHARD BLACKABY

THOMAS NELSON
Since 1798

NASHVILLE DALLAS MEXICO CITY RIO DE JANEIRO

Published in Nashville, Tennessee, by Thomas Nelson. Thomas Nelson is a registered trademark of Thomas Nelson, Inc.

Thomas Nelson, Inc., titles may be purchased in bulk for educational, business, fund-raising, or sales promotional use. For information, please e-mail SpecialMarkets@ThomasNelson.com.

All Scripture references are from THE NEW KING JAMES VERSION. © 1979, 1980, 1982, Thomas Nelson, Inc., Publishers.

Published in association with the literary agency of Wolgemuth & Associates, Inc.

ISBN: 978-0-7852-6204-6

Printed in the United States of America
04 05 06 07 VG 6 5 4 3 2 1

CONTENTS

USING THIS WORKBOOK

This workbook is a companion to our book by the same name, *Called to Be God's Leader.* We have also drawn from other sources, including various seminars on spiritual leadership we have conducted. The Scripture texts are from The New King James Version of the Bible.

The workbook is divided into ten units, and within each unit, the subject matter has been divided into five daily segments. Unit divisions generally correspond to chapters in the book, but the division of material into daily segments is unique to the workbook. We have interspersed three types of questions throughout the text:

- *Bible Contemplation*—questions related to Bible verses noted in the book

- *Personal Response*—questions that call upon your personal experience, beliefs, ideas, and opinions

- *Concept Reflection*—questions pertaining to specific statements

There are no right answers to these questions. We have provided them to stimulate your creativity and to trigger spiritual insight. They are intended to be probing, thought provoking, and spiritually challenging.

In addition, you will find two recurring features in the workbook:

- *Added Insight into Spiritual Leadership.* These are segments that are unrelated to the text of *Called to Be God's Leader* but are related to the general concepts of spiritual leadership presented in the book.

- *Another Leader in God's Word.* These are segments that illustrate key leadership principles in the lives of other Bible leaders—some of whom give examples of what *to* do and others of what *not* to do.

This workbook may be used in both individual and small-group studies. Please note, however, that not all of the questions are necessarily appropriate for group sharing. Many of the questions call for deep personal introspection.

Some questions may be more appropriately restated in objective terms for general group discussion.

Also note at the outset that questions in Unit Ten pertain primarily to each of the first nine chapters. You will find the related chapter noted at the end of each question.

UNIT I

LIMITLESS POSSIBILITIES

> *Then Moses spoke to the* LORD, *saying: "Let the* LORD, *the God of the spirits of all flesh, set a man over the congregation, who may go out before them and go in before them, who may lead them out and bring them in, that the congregation of the* LORD *may not be like sheep which have no shepherd."*
>
> *And the* LORD *said to Moses: "Take Joshua the son of Nun with you, a man in whom is the Spirit, and lay your hand on him; set him before Eleazar the priest and before all the congregation, and inaugurate him in their sight. And you shall give some of your authority to him, that all the congregation of the children of Israel may be obedient. He shall stand before Eleazar the priest, who shall inquire before the* LORD *for him by the judgment of the Urim; at his word they shall go out, and at his word they shall come in, he and all the children of Israel with him—all the congregation."*
>
> *So Moses did as the* LORD *commanded him. He took Joshua and set him before Eleazar the priest and before all the congregation. And he laid his hands on him and inaugurated him, just as the* LORD *commanded by the hand of Moses.*
>
> NUMBERS 27:15–23

Our world craves good leaders. It would seem that effective leadership has become the panacea for every challenge society faces. Whether it's politics, religion, business, education, or law, the universally expressed need is for leaders who will rise to meet the challenges that seem to overwhelm many of today's organizations.

For decades the question has been asked: "Are leaders born or are they made?" Those who believe leaders are born see leaders as having inbred personality traits and genetically predetermined talents that cause the person to gravitate toward and assume leadership roles. The born leader cannot help but lead! Those who believe leaders are made see leaders as those who receive specialized training that qualifies them for a leadership role.

God's Word takes a different approach. The Bible tells us that leaders are those whom God chooses and raises up. Those who become the most successful, admired, and positive leaders are those who have a deep relationship with God and who are elevated to a position of leadership by Him. The Bible says, "The eyes of the LORD run to and fro throughout the whole earth, to show Himself strong on behalf of those whose heart is loyal to Him" (2 Chron. 16:9). *Any* person, therefore, can qualify for a leadership position. *Any* person deeply committed to the Lord is a person whom God can raise up into a high-profile, effective leadership position.

Indeed, some of the greatest leaders in the Bible were people that others would have totally discounted, both on the basis of their past and upbringing, and on the basis of their training. They were chosen for leadership and became great leaders because their hearts were completely devoted to the Lord God. We can learn much from their examples.

One of these great leaders in the Bible whose early life bore no hint of the great man he would become was Joshua.

Joshua's forefathers were slaves. Spanning four centuries, Joshua's ancestors had lived in Egypt, much of that time in bondage. Born with no possibility of freedom, education, or military training, the thought of a stellar military career would have seemed ludicrous to Joshua. Yet he became a victorious general and, even more important, a dynamic spiritual leader. The key to Joshua's astounding career was not found in his abilities or opportunities. Nor was it in his character, though that was of sterling quality. The key was not found in Joshua at all. It was found in God. Joshua was an ordinary man who was devoted to and willingly served a great God.

Joshua had many admirable qualities, but he also had his flaws. Like everyone, he had his limitations. People, even great people, are prone to failure. They can succumb to their difficult circumstances. But words like *cannot* and *impossible* have no place in God's vocabulary (Rom. 8:31). From heaven's perspective, nothing is impossible (Luke 1:37). Likewise, when God sets a plan in motion, failure is not an option. These truths were made abundantly clear in Joshua's life despite his humble circumstances.

Joshua was an ordinary man who served a great God.

DAY ONE

GOD USED JOSHUA DESPITE HIS PAST

Details about Joshua's father are sketchy except that he was a slave from a long line of slaves. His name was Nun. Joshua's grandfather and great-grandfather were raised in bondage. It was their family business. It was all they knew. Generations of Joshua's ancestors grew up without the privileges most people take for granted. They were deprived of rights such as freedom of movement, access to education, possession of property, and respectful treatment.

Joshua's education was dictated by his position. A strong back was more useful than a keen mind. One can imagine Nun instructing his young son, "Now Joshua, you are old enough to be working with the other men. Be careful not to look an Egyptian in the eye. That will get you a lash across your back. And don't ever be caught standing idle; it makes the taskmasters furious!"

Such childhood training would lead most Israelite children to grow up with few aspirations. At best, they could hope for a life with the fewest beatings possible and, God willing, the strength to endure each day. Such a lowly beginning was hardly what one would expect for a mighty general!

BIBLE CONTEMPLATION

> ### ROMANS 8:31
> *"If God is for us, who can be against us?"*
>
> ### LUKE 1:37
> *"For with God nothing will be impossible."*

When you read the two verses above, do you see them fully applicable to *your* life? Or do you find yourself saying: *Except . . . but . . . however?*

_____ Is there something that keeps you from *fully* accepting God's possibilities for you? If so, what is it? _____

> ### 2 CHRONICLES 16:9
> *"The eyes of the LORD run to and fro throughout the whole earth, to show Himself strong on behalf of those whose heart is loyal to Him."*

On the basis of this verse what do you believe your position to be before the Lord?

_____

_____

_____

_____

Is your heart loyal to Him? _____

Joshua undoubtedly grew up well acquainted with suffering. Thousands of years before workers' rights, legal protection, or public health care, a Hebrew slave's life would have been tedious, painful, and brief. The book of Exodus describes Egypt's cruel oppression of God's people. When God enlisted Moses to be His minister of deliverance for them, God said, "I have surely seen the oppression of My people who are in Egypt, and have heard their cry because of their taskmasters, for I know their sorrows" (Ex. 3:7).

Joshua quite likely saw those he loved whipped and beaten. Perhaps he helped tend their bloodied backs and watched the adults nursing their broken bones and rubbing their aching muscles. As he looked into his countrymen's eyes, did Joshua see the distant, hollow looks of those who had long since lost any hope of their freedom? It's possible that among the sounds of moaning and weeping during the night's stillness, Joshua also overheard the hushed conversations of the adults wistfully describing their hope for the future and debating whether they would ever escape their misery.

What must have passed through young Joshua's mind as he watched the dreaded Egyptian soldiers racing past in their splendid chariots? Did Joshua remember that only a generation earlier, these soldiers had brutally massacred Hebrew babies in a crude attempt at population control? Was he mocked and mimicked by proud Egyptian boys as he passed them on the way to his work site? By the time Joshua was a teenager, he had probably been taunted with every derogatory term in the Egyptian language. While Egyptian boys dreamed of becoming war heroes, victorious generals, and world travelers, what dreams did the slave boy Joshua harbor? Everything about Joshua's world spoke of hopelessness. Yet did he dream, as young boys do, of a nobler life for himself and for his children?

PERSONAL RESPONSE

What dreams did you have for your life when you were a child? Think in terms of the quality of life you dreamed about having, rather than a specific career.

_____

_____

_____

What realities of your childhood have limited what you have done or become?

_____

_____

_____

Are you hopeful, or hopeless about your future? Explain why.

_____

_____

_____

In spite of how you *feel*, what do you believe God desires for you?

_____

_____

_____

Whatever his dreams were, in reality his future looked bleak, and his present circumstances were equally dismal. Yet his distant past must have intrigued him. Hebrew parents would regularly recite the stories of their beginnings to their children. They would recount how, centuries earlier, God had encountered Abraham and told him to move his family from Haran to the land of Canaan. The adults would describe how Abraham trusted God's promise that one day his descendants would fill that land and be as numerous as the stars in the sky.

They would relate how the revered patriarch Abraham, when he was one hundred years old, miraculously became a father. His elderly wife, Sarah, bore a son, Isaac. Isaac had two sons, Esau and Jacob. Despite Jacob's questionable beginnings, he, too, became a patriarch and God renamed him Israel. Jacob had twelve famous sons. God apparently had special plans for the eleventh son, Joseph. As a young boy, Joseph dreamed of one day being used mightily by God. Joseph's brothers grew jealous of their younger brother, so they sold him into slavery and exiled him to Egypt.

At this point in the story, young Joshua's heart must have quickened, for *he* was a descendant of Joseph. Regardless of how many times he heard the story, Joshua must have been thrilled to hear how Joseph rocketed from confinement in a dismal Egyptian prison cell all the way to an exalted and influential position at Pharaoh's right hand. When a famine forced Joseph's brothers to move their families to Egypt, Joseph became preeminent over them, just as God had foretold.

As the twelve sons of Jacob had children and enlarged their families, each of Jacob's sons' descendants became a tribe of Israel. Unlike the other tribes, however, God declared that Joseph's descendants would be so numerous as to form two tribes under his two sons, Manasseh and Ephraim. Both tribes would become powerful, but the descendants of the younger brother, Ephraim, would greatly surpass those from Manasseh's tribe. Joshua was from Ephraim's tribe.

Joseph's story would have seemed like a fairy tale to the young boys of Joshua's day. But it had happened. God had taken one of His children from the lowest position in society and elevated him to the highest. "If God did it once . . ." Surely the young Hebrew boys would argue over which tribe was the greatest as they played. They would have speculated whether the distant prophecies concerning their tribes would ever become a reality.

The aged Jacob had prophesied of Joseph's tribe:

Joseph is a fruitful bough, a fruitful bough by a well; his branches run over the wall. The archers have bitterly grieved him, shot at him and hated him. But his bow remained in strength, and the arms of his hands were made strong by the hands of the Mighty God of Jacob (from there is the Shepherd, the Stone of Israel), by the God of your father who will help you, and by the Almighty who will bless you with blessings of heaven above, blessings of the deep that lies beneath, blessings of the breasts and of the womb. The blessings of your father have excelled the blessings of my ancestors, up to the utmost bound of the everlasting hills. They shall be on the head of Joseph, and on the crown of the head of him who was separate from his brothers. (Genesis 49:22–26)

As young Joshua heard the elders reciting this prophecy, it may have seemed like a cruel joke. Yet the prophecy claimed that one day, Joseph's descendants would receive bountiful blessings from God. They would be valiant warriors with deadly bows. God Himself would strengthen the arms of their archers. Joshua was a direct descendant of the famous Joseph. Joshua knew the prophecy that his tribe, Ephraim, would one day be a mighty people (Gen. 48:19). Joshua's grandfather was Elishama, the chief of Ephraim (1 Chron. 7:26–27; Num. 1:10). Yet, despite his prominent ties to Ephraim, God's promises probably seemed as distant to Joshua as his dead ancestor Joseph.

God's promises probably seemed as distant to Joshua as his dead ancestor Joseph.

BIBLE CONTEMPLATION

JEREMIAH 29:11–13

"For I know the thoughts that I think toward you, says the LORD, thoughts of peace and not of evil, to give you a future and a hope. Then you will call upon Me and go and pray to Me, and I will listen to you. And you will seek Me and find Me, when you search for Me with all your heart."

As you read this passage, what *future and a hope* immediately come to your mind and heart?

_____

_____

What does God want to do in your life so you will have a hope for your future?

_____

_____

_____

DAY TWO

GOD USED JOSHUA DESPITE HIS YOUTH

In Joshua's day the Israelite people revered their elders. The elders made all the decisions. Joshua would have still been a young man when the Exodus began. He would not have been considered a prominent national leader. Moses and his generation were the influential ones of that day. This may explain, in part, Joshua's initial silence when he returned from spying out the land with the other eleven spies. He and Caleb were in favor of immediately occupying the land of Canaan (Num. 13:30; 14:6–10).

When the minority report was given, however, the elder Caleb initially spoke out rather than Joshua. And, when Joshua lent his voice to Caleb's pleas, rather than being persuaded, the people sought to kill him. Ironically, there would come a time when the Israelites would not question a word from Joshua, no matter how incredulous it might sound. However, in Joshua's youth this was not yet the case. Joshua still had much to learn and much to experience before the people would follow him unquestioningly. God was still shaping his young life.

Joshua still had much to learn and much to experience before the people would follow him unquestioningly.

The Bible reveals a consistent pattern wherein God revealed to young men and women His plans to use their lives in a significant way. God gave young Joseph dreams of ruling over his brothers long before that revelation became a reality (Gen. 37:5–11). Samuel was consecrated to the Lord's service even before his conception (1 Sam. 1:11).

Likewise, God appointed the prophet Jeremiah for service before he was born (Jer. 1:5). Jeremiah hesitated to serve God because he was young, but God exhorted him, "Do not say, 'I am a youth,' for you shall go to all to whom I send you, and whatever I command you, you shall speak" (Jer. 1:7).

David was still a young shepherd boy when God alerted him that one day he would be a king (1 Sam. 16:12–13). Mary was still a teenager when she learned of God's incredible plans for her future (Luke 1:26–37). John was probably a young man when Jesus called him to follow Him. As the apostle Paul mentored young Timothy, he had to encourage his youthful protégé, "Let no one despise your youth" (1 Tim. 4:12).

Historically, God has repeatedly chosen young people and fashioned them into great leaders. The key for each of them, as it would be for Joshua, was their willingness to be patient and obedient as God prepared them for His purposes. At times emerging leaders limit their future possibilities by their impatience. They look for shortcuts to success, but God is methodical. He typically lays a foundation of character before building a superstructure of leadership.

PERSONAL RESPONSE

Did God reveal His plan for you early in your life? (This may be the first time you have admitted this revelation to anyone—even to yourself.)

_____

_____

Have you, or someone you know, ever tried to take a shortcut to personal success? What was the result?

_____

_____

_____

At times emerging leaders limit their future possibilities by their impatience.

ADDED INSIGHT INTO SPIRITUAL LEADERSHIP FACTORS

RELATED TO LEADERSHIP ABILITIES

A person's leadership abilities are often influenced by factors related to the person's:

1. Home life

2. Past failures

3. Life crises and disappointments

4. Personal struggles related to physical factors, personality, or fears

Identify at least one factor for each of the above that you believe impacts your ability to lead (either positively or negatively—in other words, a factor that you believe helps you to be a leader or that has kept you from becoming the best leader you might be).

Home life factor: _____

Past failure: _____

Life crisis or disappointment: _____

Personal struggle: _____

Another pattern found in Scripture is that God often provides significant mentors, teachers, and encouragers in individuals' lives to ready them for their future assignments. The aged priest Eli prepared young Samuel. Samuel worked with Saul. Elijah instructed Elisha. Joshua's primary teacher was Moses.

There is no record of Joshua resisting Moses' leadership or resenting his instruction. Joshua apparently did not second-guess his leader. Rather, he accepted his assistant role and zealously performed his assignments. Joshua obviously had faith in God's timing. He trusted God, not just in the abstract, but in his present circumstances. Because Joshua did not lose patience with God, he lived to enjoy a rewarding future, just as God promised.

Moses was a transitional leader. God used him to lead the Israelites out of Egypt to Canaan's doorstep. Yet Moses would not lead the people into the promised land. The next phase in God's plan would call on Joshua, the one who had been faithful during the transition time. Transitional periods can be difficult, especially for the young.

Like many young people, Joshua could have grown impetuous, anxious to move on to the next stage of his career. It would have been challenging to remain faithful to God and His assignment when things were in flux. No doubt Joshua pondered whether some of Moses' decisions were best. But, to his credit and to God's glory, he chose to be patient and glean all the wisdom he could from his elders, especially Moses.

Transitional periods can be difficult, especially for the young.

PERSONAL RESPONSE

Who has God put in your life as a mentor—not only now but in the past? Identify at least one mentor, but feel free to list several. Identify one or two key lessons you learned from each person:

_____

_____

_____

Have you ever rebelled against something your mentors tried to teach you? What were the results?

_____

_____

_____

Have you ever been impatient, anxious to move to the next stage of your career but unable to do so? What do you believe God may have been trying to teach you during that time?

_____

_____

_____

CONCEPT REFLECTION

CONCEPT: God is not as interested in our origins as He is in our obedience.

God is not as interested in our origins as He is in our obedience.

What do you believe might be the purpose for the origins God gave you?

_____

_____

_____

DAY THREE

GOD USED JOSHUA DESPITE THE SINS OF OTHERS

Joshua's early life could be viewed from the perspective of abandonment. Many of the most significant people in his life left him. We must glean this in part from the silence of Scripture. Joshua's father, Nun, though named, is never described. There is no record of him teaching Joshua or giving him advice the way Moses' father-in-law counseled him (Ex. 18:13–27). We don't know if Nun was alive at the time of the Exodus. We can only assume that under the harsh working conditions, the life span of slaves was cruelly brief.

Did Joshua's father die while Joshua was still a young man, as Jesus' earthly father, Joseph, did? Could that be why God led Moses to adopt him as his successor, bypassing Moses' own sons? If this is true, then God's work in Joshua's life is even more telling, since Joshua may have lacked the nurture and support of a father during some of the most critical days of his young life.

It is possible that Nun was alive during the Exodus. If so, this poses another problem, for Nun's generation committed a great sin against God by not trusting Him to lead them into the promised land. There is no record of Joshua's father speaking up in support of his son and Caleb after the twelve spies returned. This could indicate that either Nun had died by that time, or he was among those who lacked faith in God.

If Nun was among the unfaithful generation, then Joshua would have had to suffer the anguish of wandering in the wilderness for forty years waiting for his own father to die, along with the other elders. Only then could Joshua move forward again. Seemingly either scenario—losing his father at a young age, or having an unbelieving father—meant Joshua had to rely upon the Lord for his guidance and strength in his faith.

Interestingly, Jesus lost His earthly father, Joseph, at a relatively young age. By the time Jesus entered His adult ministry, His father had apparently died and the only father Jesus could turn to was His Father in heaven.

A substantial number of history's famous leaders rose to greatness with little or no parental support, including Alexander the Great, Winston Churchill, Horatio Nelson, the Duke of Wellington, and George Washington. It is true that parental love and support are critical for a healthy upbringing, but God promises to be a "father of the fatherless" (Ps. 68:5). Joshua did not have many faithful role models among the elders and leaders of his people.

BIBLE CONTEMPLATION

> ### PSALM 68:5
> *"A father of the fatherless, a defender of widows, is God in His holy habitation."*

In what ways has God been a father to you, perhaps in an area of life in which one or both of your earthly parents seemed to fail—for whatever reason—to be a good parent? (Note that God's nuturing of you may have occurred when you were an adult, even more so than when you were a child.)

_____

_____

_____

_____

If anyone could have trusted God for miracles, it should have been the Hebrew leaders. They had seen God's fearsome ten plagues bring the mighty Egyptian empire to its knees. They had crossed the dry bed of the Red Sea and then watched the waters return to engulf the pursuing Egyptian army.

God had led them across the desert using a cloud by day and a pillar of fire at night. God miraculously provided daily food and water for an entire nation. Surely no generation ever witnessed such a spectacular array of miracles! Yet, when the twelve spies returned from staking out the promised land, the majority reported:

"We are not able to go up against the people, for they are stronger than we." And they gave the children of Israel a bad report of the land which they had spied out, saying, "The land through which we have gone as spies is a land that devours its inhabitants, and all the people whom we saw in it are men of great stature. There we saw the giants (the descendants of Anak came from the giants); and we were like grasshoppers in our own sight, and so we were in their sight." (Numbers 13:31–33)

BIBLE CONTEMPLATION

NUMBERS 13:31–33

"We are not able to go up against the people, for they are stronger than we . . . We were like grasshoppers in our own sight, and so we were in their sight."

Had you been one of the twelve spies, what do you think your response would have been?

_____

_____

_____

_____

_____

Why do you think you would have taken that position?

_____

_____

_____

_____

> ### 1 CORINTHIANS 1:26–27
> *"For you see your calling, brethren, that not many wise according to the flesh, not many mighty, not many noble, are called. But God has chosen the foolish things of the world to put to shame the wise, and God has chosen the weak things of the world to put to shame the things which are mighty."*

How do you believe God might use your *weakness* to demonstrate His strength?

_____

_____

_____

> ### 2 CORINTHIANS 12:9–10
> *"And He said to me, 'My grace is sufficient for you, for My strength is made perfect in weakness.' Therefore most gladly I will rather boast in my infirmities, that the power of Christ may rest upon me. Therefore I take pleasure in infirmities, in reproaches, in needs, in persecutions, in distresses, for Christ's sake. For when I am weak, then I am strong."*

In what ways have you found yourself to be weak in yourself and yet strong in Christ?

_____

_____

_____

_____

How difficult and in what ways do you find it a challenge to *take pleasure* in infirmities, reproaches, needs, persecutions, and distresses for Christ's sake?

_____

_____

_____

_____

From that point on, things unraveled for the Israelites. The people degenerated to the point of worshiping a golden calf Aaron made for them out of their own jewelry. This generation composed the nation's leaders as Joshua emerged into adulthood. How easy it could have been for Joshua to embrace the faithless attitudes prevalent among the influential elders. He would have heard them discussing and justifying their desertion of God. Perhaps Joshua's own relatives were effusive in their reasons why God's will was impossible to follow.

Israel was not without its faithful spiritual leaders, but even they struggled. Moses, Joshua's revered leader, disqualified himself from entering the promised land when he succumbed to his anger and disobeyed God's explicit command (Num. 20:1–13). Aaron and Miriam, two of God's most steadfast followers during Joshua's young adulthood, also paid a price for their disobedience. They had not been blameless, and they would suffer the consequences (Num. 12; 20:22–29). It must have disheartened Joshua to see his spiritual leaders fall by the wayside along with the rest of their generation. The indomitable Caleb would be the only elder to enter the promised land with Joshua.

Where did this leave Joshua? Those he had been raised to honor and respect were waffling in their faith and obedience. And, looking at the situation from a human perspective, they had good reason for their reluctance. Compared to the Canaanites, they were like "grasshoppers." Joshua had seen the terrifying enemy with his own eyes. Yet he chose to go against the prevailing consensus. Why? Perhaps he understood, like the apostle Paul, that one day he would give an account to almighty God for what *he* had done, and therefore he followed his convictions, even if he stood alone (2 Cor. 5:10).

The Scriptures honor many men and women who, like Joshua, found themselves virtually alone in their obedience. Imagine being Noah, the only righteous person left on earth (Gen. 6:8)! Lot was the sole godly person living in Sodom (Gen. 19:15). Esther was the only believer in the king's household (Est. 2:10). Micaiah was the only prophet in Israel who prophesied what God told him rather than what the king wanted to hear (1 Kings 22:8). Job stood alone against the counsel of his friends and even his own wife. Such men and women are heroes of the faith, not because of any great performance of their own, but because they had the courage and good sense to trust God even as those around them did not. Joshua was one of those heroes.

PERSONAL RESPONSE

Have you ever felt alone or isolated in your obedience to God? Cite a specific example.

> **How easy it could have been for Joshua to embrace the faithless attitudes prevalent among the influential elders.**

> **He followed his convictions, even if he stood alone.**

_____

_____

What can a period of isolated obedience do to a person's faith?

_____

_____

_____

Thanks to the Israelites' lack of faith, Joshua spent forty years wandering with them in the wilderness. Imagine what went through Joshua's mind when he heard God's edict pronounced to the people:

> "As I live," says the LORD, "just as you have spoken in My hearing, so I will do to you: The carcasses of you who have complained against Me shall fall in this wilderness, all of you who were numbered, according to your entire number, from twenty years old and above. Except for Caleb the son of Jephunneh and Joshua the son of Nun, you shall by no means enter the land which I swore I would make you dwell in. But your little ones, whom you said would be victims, I will bring in, and they shall know the land which you have despised. But as for you, your carcasses shall fall in this wilderness. And your sons shall be shepherds in the wilderness forty years, and bear the brunt of your infidelity, until your carcasses are consumed in the wilderness. According to the number of the days in which you spied out the land, forty days, for each day you shall bear your guilt one year, namely forty years, and you shall know My rejection. I the LORD have spoken this. I will surely do so to all this evil congregation who are gathered together against Me. In this wilderness they shall be consumed, and there they shall die." (Numbers 14:28–35)

God certainly did not break the news gently! The Israelites, of all people, should have been primed to obey God. He had shown His power to them in every way imaginable, proving His trustworthiness. Now His words of reprimand to them were devastating. How heart wrenching to hear that God's will for you is for you to die! How pathetic the wails and sobs would have sounded as they rang out across the desert.

Surely Joshua was moved to see his uncles and aunts weeping under the weight of God's punishment on them. How pitiful it must have looked as the recalcitrant Hebrews strapped on their swords the next morning, determined to do, albeit belatedly, what God had told them to do in the first place. Despite Moses' warnings that neither he nor God would go with them, they foolishly assumed that since they were now ready to obey God's command, God would reverse His judgment upon them.

They were about to learn a difficult lesson: people leave God on their terms, but they return on God's terms. Joshua must have watched with heavy heart as the humiliated Israelite survivors trudged back into camp, soundly defeated by the Amalekites and the Canaanites (Num. 14:39–45).

CONCEPT REFLECTION

Have you, or someone you know, ever left God? In what ways did you return on *God's* terms?

_____

_____

_____

> **People leave God on their terms, but they return on God's terms.**

DAY FOUR

GOD USED A TRANSITION TIME IN JOSHUA'S LIFE

We cannot underestimate the profound impact wandering forty years in the wilderness would have had on Joshua. He had been ready and willing to enter the promised land immediately. But, because of someone else's sin, Joshua would have to delay God's will for his own life by forty years. This could have been an unproductive and wasted time, but Joshua chose to spend it walking with God, and time spent with God is never wasted.

Joshua experienced four decades of life lessons as he lived through the punishment alongside the guilty ones. Could there have been any more graphic lesson on the perils of disobeying God? For forty years Joshua witnessed firsthand the consequences of disobedience. Joshua would attend burial after burial, knowing what might have been had that person only trusted the Lord. As even the great leaders Aaron, Miriam, and Moses all remained outside the promised land, Joshua must have determined in his heart to never accept less than God's best for his life.

PERSONAL RESPONSE

Have you ever watched others suffer the consequences of their disobedience or rebellion against God? Focus on a specific experience. How did you feel?

_____

_____

_____

How did their disobedience impact your life?

_____

_____

_____

How did you respond?

_____

_____

_____

As he paid the price for their sin, Joshua could not have helped but contemplate the failures of his predecessors. Did Joshua seek times of solitude in the desert, trying to understand why God would deal so severely with disobedience? What about Moses? Such a mighty man of God, yet he, too, was punished for his disobedience and irreverence. Could Joshua escape the truth that no person, not even one used to part the Red Sea, was exempt from accountability to almighty, holy God?

Did Joshua develop a prayer life during those wilderness wanderings that would be his lifeline to God when he was leading the army? Did Joshua use that time to develop the personal habits of meditation and moral purity that would characterize his later life? Did God clearly and unmistakably assure Joshua of His purposes for him during that time?

Whereas Moses argued and resisted God's will for him, Joshua appeared to have a stolid resolve throughout his time of leadership. Could it be that after communing with God for forty years in the wilderness, all his doubts and concerns were resolved? Clearly Joshua did not waste this time. While others were merely passing their days, Joshua emerged as a national leader. After four decades he was well prepared to boldly lead his people against numerous and seemingly insurmountable challenges.

PERSONAL RESPONSE

Does your life seem to be on hold because of the actions of another person or group of people? Identify several positive and godly things you might do to make the most of this time.

_____

_____

> **For forty years Joshua witnessed firsthand the consequences of disobedience.**

ADDED INSIGHT INTO
SPIRITUAL LEADERSHIP

COMMON PITFALLS

There are at least ten common pitfalls that cause spiritual leaders to fail:

1. Pride—including taking all the credit for an organization's success, and at times, for what God has done or is doing

2. Sexual sin

3. Cynicism—which is an indication that a leader's focus has shifted from the goodness and greatness of God to the errors and human foibles of people

4. Greed—yielding to the lure of material possessions and money at the expense of obeying God's will

5. Mental laziness—refusing to grow as a leader, stay abreast of situations, and follow through on the directions given by the Holy Spirit

6. Oversensitivity—to criticism, being second-guessed, and having motives questioned

7. Spiritual lethargy—allowing daily commitments to crowd out their time with Christ

8. Domestic neglect—failing to make their families a priority in their giving of time and affection

9. Administrative carelessness—focusing so much on the greater vision that they neglect building the people and policies that can lead an organization to achieve the vision . . . often evidenced by a lack of communication both bottom-to-top and top-to-bottom

10. Prolonged position holding—not knowing when the time has come to transition to successors

As you have read through this list, which of these pitfalls have stood out to you in a convicting, troubling way?

_____

_____

_____

_____

What might you do, beginning today, to overcome this pitfall?

_____

_____

_____

DAY FIVE

GOD ALLOWS US TO CHOOSE

Some people inherit leadership positions. Others earn them. Joshua was certainly one of the latter. Nothing came easy for him. Joshua's initial slavery was not caused by his own failure, but by the decisions others had made centuries earlier. Likewise, Joshua's long years in the desert were not penance for his own sin, but payment for others' failures. A lesser man would have become bitter, but Joshua was wiser than that.

He couldn't always choose his circumstances but he could choose his response to them. Wise leaders refuse to let crises crush them. They use obstacles for their advantage. Times of waiting can be agonizing for a leader. Joshua made the most of his transition time. He didn't squander the years muttering about missed opportunities. He seized the opportunities God granted him. Most important, he never neglected his own walk with God. Because of his faithfulness he retained his hope.

Some people inherit leadership positions. Others earn them.

PERSONAL RESPONSE

Are you making the most of the present circumstances in your life? What do you think God wants to do to make you a better person at the conclusion of this time?

_____

_____

_____

What is God teaching you during this time?

_____

_____

_____

_____

Added Insight into Spiritual Leadership

Three Things That Never Change

There are three things that never change in any situation, work environment, family, or circumstance:

1. God does not change. He remains the same, without variation (James 1:17). You can trust Him to be the same yesterday, today, and forever (Heb. 13:8).

2. The world of unbelievers does not change. Technology may have changed through the years, but the human heart has remained the same. Those who do not know the Lord live in darkness. They are enslaved by the same enemy and the same power structures as ungodly people throughout the ages (John 3:19).

3. The people of God remain the same. They are sheep who need both the Good Shepherd and a human shepherd who will lead them to Christ.

Evaluate the frustrations you may have experienced—feeling perhaps that God has changed, people in the world *should* be different than they are, or that Christians should behave in ways they aren't behaving. How do you need to change *your* perspective in the light that God, unbelievers and the world as a whole, and the people of God as a whole, behave in familiar patterns?

_____

_____

_____

Joshua faced hardships and disappointments mostly foreign to us, yet he allowed God to interpret those circumstances for him. He faced the same travails that caused the demise of thousands of others, but he grew stronger as a result.

We have the opportunity to do the same thing. Success does not hinge on our heredity but on our heavenly Father. It does not depend on what others do but on what *we* choose to do. An effective life is not a matter of golden opportunities and lucky breaks. True success is determined by how we respond to the circumstances God allows us to experience.

God can use your life significantly, just as He used Joshua's. The question is: Are you prepared to let Him?

CONCEPT REFLECTION

CONCEPT: **True success is determined by how we respond to the circumstances God allows us to experience.**

What is your definition of a successful response to life's circumstances—both good and bad?

_____

_____

_____

_____

_____

ADDED INSIGHT INTO SPIRITUAL LEADERSHIP

WHAT DOES *LEADERSHIP* MEAN?

Read through the following three commonly held definitions of *leadership*. Below each statement, state why you disagree or agree:

1. Leadership is the process of persuading others to follow the objectives of a leader.

_____

_____

_____

2. Leadership is influence.

_____

_____

_____

3. Leadership is the mobilization of resources in order to arouse or spur on motives that followers already have.

_____

_____

_____

In what ways does it make a difference in your response to the leadership statements above if you acknowledge that God only honors leadership that reflects loyalty to Him?

_____

_____

_____

_____

_____

Is there a distinct difference in the way Christians are to manifest leadership, in comparison to those who are not Christians? If not, why not? If so, how so?

_____

_____

_____

_____

_____

UNIT 2

SEIZING MOMENTS
TO BE FAITHFUL

Now Amalek came and fought with Israel in Rephidim. And Moses said to Joshua, "Choose us some men and go out, fight with Amalek. Tomorrow I will stand on the top of the hill with the rod of God in my hand." So Joshua did as Moses said to him, and fought with Amalek. And Moses, Aaron, and Hur went up to the top of the hill. And so it was, when Moses held up his hand, that Israel prevailed; and when he let down his hand, Amalek prevailed . . . So Joshua defeated Amalek and his people with the edge of the sword.

EXODUS 17:8–11, 13

Then the Commander of the LORD's army said to Joshua, "Take your sandal off your foot, for the place where you stand is holy." And Joshua did so.

JOSHUA 5:15

As the LORD had commanded Moses his servant, so Moses commanded Joshua, and so Joshua did. He left nothing undone of all that the LORD had commanded Moses.

JOSHUA 11:15

Some aspiring leaders constantly seek "the big break." They distribute their résumés, applying for important and prestigious positions. They use political tactics to gain friends and forge alliances. Sadly, those seeking to serve God often follow the same pattern. In so doing, they neglect the most basic lesson in spiritual leadership: if you are faithful in a little, God will entrust you with more (Matt. 25:21; Luke 16:10).

The most basic lesson in spiritual leadership: if you are faithful in a little, God will entrust you with more.

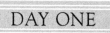

Joshua: A Faithful Life

Faithfulness was fundamental to Joshua's success. More important, God was the key to Joshua's success. God relates to people on the basis of a covenant or promise. God said He would respond to obedience in one way and to disobedience in another (Deut. 27:11–28:68). When people trust in Him, He rewards their faithfulness, sometimes in miraculous ways. When people refuse to believe Him, they miss out on what God would have done and they face His discipline.

Only God knows what *could* have been with Joshua's peers had they obeyed God's revealed will for them. But Joshua was different. He was faithful so he experienced God's hand of blessing and power in everything he did. Step by step, Joshua's obedience led him to the top leadership position of his nation.

Bible Contemplation

Matthew 25:21

"His lord said to him, 'Well done, good and faithful servant; you were faithful over a few things, I will make you ruler over many things. Enter into the joy of your lord.'"

Luke 16:10

"He who is faithful in what is least is faithful also in much; and he who is unjust in what is least is unjust also in much."

Is it more difficult to trust God with little or with much? Why?

_____

_____

_____

Concept Reflection

CONCEPT: **When people trust in God, He rewards their faithfulness, sometimes in miraculous ways. When people refuse to believe Him, they miss out on what God would have done and they face His discipline.**

As you reflect on your own life or the life of someone you know, can you see these principles at work? Cite a specific example:

_____

_____

_____

_____

_____

_____

Joshua did not apply to be Moses' assistant. God chose him. When Moses asked God who should lead the people, God appointed Joshua:

> Then Moses spoke to the LORD, saying: "Let the LORD, the God of the spirits of all flesh, set a man over the congregation, who may go out before them and go in before them, who may lead them out and bring them in, that the congregation of the LORD may not be like sheep which have no shepherd." And the LORD said to Moses: "Take Joshua the son of Nun with you, a man in whom is the Spirit, and lay your hand on him; set him before Eleazar the priest and before all the congregation, and inaugurate him in their sight. And you shall give some of your authority to him, that all the congregation of the children of Israel may be obedient." (Numbers 27:15–21)

Joshua never set out to climb the ladder of success, nor did he pursue a career path in leadership. He did not assess his giftedness and decide on a military career. He served Moses because that was God's assignment for him. The initiative came from God. This truth would sustain Joshua during the darkest days when leading God's people was exceedingly difficult.

Many people of our generation scheme and plan to improve their positions. They are commended as "industrious." They carefully monitor their salaries and benefits to ensure they receive maximum return for their efforts. They are viewed as good money managers. They may achieve prominent positions, but these come through their own efforts.

While they may take pride in their own achievements, they will never know the influence or satisfaction that comes from knowing God has appointed them to their positions. Joshua's life could certainly be labeled a success story, but his success was not hard won. It was God given. The same is true of people like Joseph, Daniel, and David. They achieved significant success—even measuring by worldly standards—but they didn't do it the world's way.

His success was not "hard won." It was God given.

PERSONAL RESPONSE

Do you believe God has appointed you to the position you are in today? Why?

_____

_____

_____

ANOTHER LEADER
IN GOD'S WORD

SAMUEL: HONORING AND HONORED

The Bible reveals a consistent pattern in the way God relates to His people: "Those who honor Me I will honor, and those who despise Me shall be lightly esteemed" (1 Sam. 2:30). Eli the priest dishonored the Lord by the way he led his family, and God rejected him in favor of Samuel. The Bible tells us, "Samuel grew in stature, and in favor both with the LORD and men" (1 Sam. 2:26). In turn, God honored Samuel as long as Samuel honored Him. We are told "the LORD was with him and let none of his words fall to the ground" (1 Sam. 3:19). Whatever Samuel declared about God's promises, happened. Samuel refused to demand respect from the people, but he was greatly venerated. He honored God in both word and deed.

What does it mean to "honor God"?

_____

_____

Can you give an example of someone you know who has honored God and, in turn, been honored by God with a position of spiritual leadership?

_____

_____

_____

JOSHUA:
FAITHFUL FROM THE BEGINNING

First jobs can be quite telling. Emerging leaders don't often possess the expertise and skills experience will bring, but the attitude they bring to their first tasks can foreshadow how they will handle later responsibilities. Joshua's first major assignment was to lead the Israelite army against the hated Amalekites.

Amalek was Esau's grandson, born to Eliphaz and his concubine Timna (Gen. 36:12, 16). Esau had flatly rejected God's call on his life. Amalek chose the same path, with a vengeance. The nomadic Amalekites became the Israelites' archenemies. As the children of Israel traveled toward Canaan, the Amalekites attacked them.

Their assault was particularly odious because the Amalekites did not attack outright. Rather, they waited until the Israelites were exhausted from travel, then they ambushed the stragglers at the rear of the procession. Cutting down the weak and helpless was viewed as particularly cruel (Deut. 25:17–19). In response, Moses directed Joshua to mobilize soldiers and counterattack (Ex. 17:8–16). "So Joshua did as Moses said to him" (Ex. 17:10).

CONCEPT REFLECTION

CONCEPT: Emerging leaders don't often possess the expertise and skills experience will bring, but the attitude they bring to their first tasks can foreshadow how they will handle later responsibilities.

Cite an example in which this has been true in your life or the life of someone you know:

_____

_____

_____

Moses surveyed the skirmish from the crest of a hill as Joshua led the assault against the enemy. As long as Moses held up his arms in intercession for Joshua and his forces, the Israelites prevailed (Ex. 17:11). When Moses' arms grew weary and he was forced to lower them, the Amalekites gained the advantage. God provided a wonderful picture of an older statesman undergirding an emerging leader. As young Joshua fought his first battle, his mentor looked on, interceding for him with all his strength.

Once the battle was won, Moses built an altar and named it "The-LORD-Is-My-Banner" (Ex. 17:15). Moses was signifying that God had fought for them against their enemies. Joshua had successfully completed his first major assignment, and he had come to know indeed what it meant for God to intervene on his behalf. Centuries later these same Amalekites would be the undoing of another young leader, King Saul, because Saul chose to disobey God's directive (1 Sam. 15; 2 Sam. 1:13–16).

As young Joshua fought his first battle, his mentor looked on, interceding for him with all his strength.

JOSHUA:
FAITHFUL TO HIS NAME

In Old Testament times, a Jewish person's name was significant because it was considered a reflection of one's character. The Scriptures show that when God personally encountered people, He often changed their names to reflect His will for them. Abram and Sarai became Abraham and Sarah to signify that God would establish a nation through them (Gen. 17:5, 15).

Jacob's new name was *Israel*, meaning "God strives," to match God's work in his life (Gen. 32:28). Rather than remaining a trickster and a conniver, he would become a patriarch of God's people. Jesus changed Simon's name to *Peter*, "a rock," to match the sturdy character God would develop in him (John 1:42).

While a name change often signaled an immediate role change, it did not automatically mean an instant alteration in character. That would come through obedience, as individuals allowed God to stretch them to match their new identities. For example, the Bible indicates that by name, Christians are children of God, yet not every Christian behaves like God's heir (Rom. 8:14–17). The degree to which Christians assume the characteristics of their new identity is up to every believer. Likewise, the Bible refers to those redeemed by Christ as saints (Rom. 1:7). But living a saintly life is a choice each Christian makes personally. A new title does not ensure a new character—obedience does.

BIBLE CONTEMPLATION

> ### ROMANS 1:7
> *"To all who are in Rome, beloved of God, called to be saints."*

Do you believe you are a saint? Why?

_____

_____

_____

_____

_____

Identify several of the character and behavioral traits you believe God desires in you:

CHARACTER TRAITS   BEHAVIORAL TRAITS

_____   _____

_____   _____

_____   _____

_____   _____

_____   _____

_____   _____

It was a highly meaningful act when God altered someone's name. When God renamed Joshua (from Hoshea), the difference was significant (Num. 13:16). *Hoshea,* meaning "He has saved," was a good, respectable name. *Joshua* meant "Yahweh saves."

God moved from generalities to specifics. *Hoshea* did not refer to a particular god. In an age of rampant idolatry, the name could have referred to any of the numerous false gods. But *Joshua* specified the one Lord God. It was personal. And indeed, Joshua would come to experience God in an increasingly personal way. The name change was subtle, but the difference was profound. *Hoshea* had a religion. *Joshua* had a relationship with God. For the rest of his life, Joshua pursued God's call to a relationship rather than merely becoming a religious leader.

PERSONAL RESPONSE

What does it mean that God has called you to a relationship with Himself?

_____

_____

_____

Use several words or phrases to describe your relationship with God:

_____

_____

_____

For the rest of his life, Joshua pursued God's call to a relationship rather than merely becoming a religious leader.

ADDED INSIGHT INTO
SPIRITUAL LEADERSHIP

RELATIONSHIP

All of the calls of God to spiritual leadership are calls to *relationship*, both with Himself and with others. In 1 Samuel 2:35 we read these sobering words: "I will raise up for Myself a faithful priest who shall do according to what is in My heart and in My mind." A priest's role was to be in relationship with God, and to work in relationship with people so *they* might enter into the fullness of a relationship with God. "But I'm not a priest," you may be saying. From God's perspective, all godly leaders function in this role whether they are working in a church, a home, a secular business, or a volunteer organization. As God's leaders, we must have an intimate relationship with God—knowing in our hearts what God is doing and revealing for the sake of His people, and then working with people to build relationships that are honoring to God and that bring people into closer relationship with God. Godly leadership is all about relationships, far more so than tasks or administrative duties!

How would you evaluate your relationship with God?

_____

_____

_____

In what ways are you in relationship with people to bring them closer to God and to each other?

_____

_____

_____

A leadership position without corresponding character inevitably leads to failure.

It is tragic whenever people pour their efforts into achievement rather than into their relationship with God. A leadership position without corresponding character inevitably leads to failure. Joshua built a relationship with God rather than a career and as a result, people are still studying his life and influence thousands of years later.

ANOTHER LEADER IN GOD'S WORD

ABRAHAM: CHARACTER OVER TIME

Abraham was one hundred years old when Isaac was born. He had waited twenty-five years for God to carry out His promise to give him an heir. What was God doing during those years? Building Abraham's character! The truth is, character building can be a slow, sometimes painful process. But the person willing to allow God to complete the process will know the joy of being used by God.

Character building takes time. There are no shortcuts.

As Abraham waited for the fulfillment of God's promises to him, he learned an important lesson about the difference between God's timing and people's timing. God sees things from an eternal perspective. People see things from a temporal view. Spiritual leaders court disaster when they panic and assume they must take matters into their own hands. When spiritual leaders wait patiently on the Lord, regardless of how long it takes, God always proves Himself absolutely true to His word. In the end, a promise fulfilled by God is always worth the wait.

Many more leaders would see major accomplishments occur in their lives and in their organizations if only they were willing to wait as long as necessary to see God accomplish His will.

What challenges have you faced in waiting for God to accomplish His plans for your life? _____

_____

In ten words or less, describe your own degree or quality of patience (or lack of patience).

_____

_____

DAY THREE

JOSHUA: A FAITHFUL BELIEVER

Leaders' reputations are not based solely upon what they *do*. What they choose *not* to do matters too.

When the Israelites reached Mount Sinai, Moses took Joshua with him up the mountain for an unforgettable experience (Ex. 24:13; 32:17–18). Scripture indicates "the glory of the LORD rested on Mount Sinai . . . the sight of the glory of the LORD was like a consuming fire" (Ex. 24:16–17). Back at the foot of the mountain, Aaron and Hur were in charge for forty days while Moses and Joshua were gone (Ex. 24:14). During Moses and Joshua's sacred encounter with God, God gave Moses the Ten Commandments. He also laid out detailed instructions concerning proper worship and sanctified behavior.

Meanwhile, without their leader, those who remained behind grew restless and agitated. One of the greatest failures in biblical history unfolded as the Hebrews exhorted Aaron, God's priest, to make them a god they could see and worship. He reluctantly took their gold and fashioned it into a golden calf (Ex. 32:1–6). In spite of witnessing God's mighty judgments on their enemies and after experiencing His miraculous provision themselves, the Israelites willingly abandoned the true, living God for a lifeless statue. What an incredible affront to almighty God!

The contrast between Aaron and Joshua is telling. We never read of Joshua bowing to the people's pressure. Aaron, however, seems to have been easily swayed. When ten of the twelve spies argued against entering the promised land, there is no record of Aaron speaking in favor of obeying God, as Joshua did, yet Aaron was God's appointed spokesman (Ex. 4:14–16). He was a gifted speaker. One could imagine him rousing the crowds to do what was right, much as Demosthenes brilliantly exhorted his fellow Athenians or Cicero challenged his Roman countrymen. But Aaron apparently remained silent when he should have pointed the people back to God.

Conversely, Joshua is not portrayed as an eloquent orator, yet he never failed to speak up as a spokesman for God. The truth is, eloquence without obedience is worthless. In fact, it's dangerous. God proved through Joshua and through countless other great leaders that a willing spirit is what He looks for when doing His mighty work. Perhaps Joshua's awareness that he was *not* a gifted speaker led him to rely completely on the Lord and, thus, to be such an effective leader.

PERSONAL RESPONSE

Is there a weakness that seems to compel you, or someone you know, to rely on God more? Explain:

_____

_____

_____

_____

_____

Eloquence without obedience is worthless. In fact, it's dangerous.

Name some reasons it might be difficult for a strong or highly accomplished person to rely on God:

_____

_____

_____

CONCEPT REFLECTION

CONCEPT: Eloquence without obedience is worthless. In fact, it's dangerous.

Have you experienced this? Give a specific example:

_____

_____

_____

Why did God allow Joshua to accompany Moses up the mountain (Ex. 24:12–13)? Did the aged Moses need Joshua to care for him as he met with God? Whether or not Moses needed Joshua, God must have wanted Joshua to experience a life-changing encounter with Him as Moses did. Joshua would need an intimate walk with God to carry out the enormous assignment awaiting him.

God gives assignments to those who have the character to handle them. God had an incredibly challenging assignment for Joshua so He fashioned his character accordingly, partly through Joshua's presence on the mount. That profound moment on the mountaintop set the tone for a lifelong intimacy between God and Joshua.

Every encounter with God opens up limitless possibilities. No one leaves an encounter with God unchanged. Certainly Joshua did not. Perhaps the sound of God's voice rang in Joshua's ears for the rest of his life. Did Joshua often recall the fire, thunder, lightning, and smoke that engulfed the mountain during those terrifying days? Did the experience so overwhelm Joshua that he could never doubt God afterward? Did the encounter so terrify Joshua that he feared God's wrath until the day he died?

> **God gives assignments to those who have the character to handle them.**

PERSONAL RESPONSE

Have you, or someone you know, had a life-changing or watershed encounter with God? Be specific. Compare and contrast the before and after:

_____

_____

Undoubtedly, Joshua's divine meeting on Mount Sinai was a watershed experience that defined the rest of his life. His presence with Moses provided this opportunity, and his absence from among the rebellious Israelites saved him from the ungodly turn of events unfolding at the base of the mountain.

Sometimes where we are *not* is as important as where we *are*. Had Joshua been among the rebellious Israelites, it seems doubtful he would have compromised his faith as Aaron did. He might have once again stood firm against the tide of apostasy. He might even have been martyred for his righteous stand. Aaron's resolve proved insufficient in his time of testing.

Soon it would be Joshua's turn to rise up as a spiritual statesman, but this time, instead of testing his faith, God was profoundly strengthening it. None of us know how often God has spared us in a similar way, but sometimes hindsight affords the wisdom to look back and thank God for preserving us from temptation and tragedy.

PERSONAL RESPONSE

Has God ever spared you from a time of temptation and tragedy? Describe a specific experience:

_____

_____

_____

How did you respond to that experience?

_____

_____

_____

Did you make any changes in your behavior as a result?

_____

_____

_____

Joshua always knew God had called him for a special purpose—to serve Him and to bring honor to His name. And Joshua spent a lifetime doing exactly that. As

> **Sometimes where we are *not* is as important as where we *are*.**

a result, he lived in a way that always demonstrated his absolute trust in God and always brought glory to God.

DAY FOUR

JOSHUA: FAITHFUL IN THE MINORITY

The Israelites were camped at Kadesh Barnea, bordering on the promised land. It was time for a reconnaissance mission to survey the territory before their initial attack (Num. 13:1–2). Under God's instructions, Moses chose one influential leader from each tribe for this momentous enterprise. It says much about Joshua that he was selected (Num. 13:8). Ephraim was a populous tribe; a large number of ambitious young men and respected older leaders were no doubt prepared to take on the assignment.

This was an exciting but dangerous mission. The land was allegedly occupied by malevolent giants. Large, formidable fortresses guarded the main roads. Capture, torture, and death were all distinct possibilities. The mission was also of great strategic significance. The twelve spies would gather critical information to determine which route the invading Israelites would take in their conquest. The nation's future rested on the success of a dozen scouts.

Of course, the spies' report is infamous now. First, they confirmed Canaan was everything God promised: "We went to the land where you sent us. It truly flows with milk and honey, and this is its fruit" (Num. 13:27). They were, to a man, impressed with the land, but ten of them were intimidated by what else they saw:

> Nevertheless the people who dwell in the land are strong; the cities are fortified and very large; moreover we saw the descendants of Anak there. The Amalekites dwell in the land of the South; the Hittites, the Jebusites, and the Amorites dwell in the mountains; and the Canaanites dwell by the sea and along the banks of the Jordan. (Numbers 13:28–29)

Yes, the land was beautiful, but immense obstacles loomed before them. These men had personally witnessed God's terrifying plagues on Egypt; they had watched God engulf the mighty Egyptian army with the Red Sea; they had seen God defeat the Amalekites en route; and they had miraculously received nourishment in the wilderness. Yet they doubted God's ability to give them victory this time.

In spite of a national history permeated with the mighty acts of God, ten of the spies assessed their situation from a human perspective. Their fear convinced them that conquering Canaan was impossible. It is a familiar pattern. Centuries later, Jesus would chastise His twelve disciples for their inability to trust Him in spite of all they had seen Him do: "'Do you not yet perceive nor understand? Is your heart still hardened? Having eyes, do you not see? And having ears, do you not hear? And do you not remember?' So He said to them, 'How is it you do not understand?'" (Mark 8:17–18, 21).

And so it was that ten of Israel's most respected leaders expressed their own unbridled fears, and the result was pandemic. The people trembled in terror. As if to seal the matter, the spies reiterated: "The land through which we have gone as spies is a land that devours its inhabitants, and all the people whom we saw in it are men of great stature. There we saw the giants . . . and we were like grasshoppers in our own sight, and so we were in their sight" (Num. 13:32–33).

At this even the most stouthearted elders and warriors lost heart. It is not surprising that God later commanded Israelite military leaders to send home any soldier who was fearful of the enemy, lest their cowardice infect their fellow soldiers (Deut. 20:8).

PERSONAL RESPONSE

Can you cite an incident in your life, or in the life of someone you know, in which *optimism* became infectious in a group of people? What was the result of that optimism?

Can you cite an incident in your life, or in the life of someone you know, in which *pessimism* became infectious in a group of people? What was the result of that pessimism?

The tremor of fright spread through the mob like a prairie-grass fire. They were united as one desperate voice in their shared anguish. Somehow, Caleb managed to quiet the crowd:

"Let us go up at once and take possession, for we are well able to overcome it" Joshua and Caleb pleaded . . . "The land we passed through to spy out is an exceedingly good land. If the LORD delights in us, then He will bring us into this land and give it to us, 'a land which flows with milk and honey.' Only do not rebel against the LORD, nor fear the people of the land, for they are our bread; their protection has departed from them, and the LORD is with us. Do not fear them." (Numbers 13:30; 14:7–9)

BIBLE CONTEMPLATION

> ### NUMBERS 14:9
> *"Do not rebel against the LORD, nor fear the people of the land."*

How difficult is it to do this?

_____

_____

_____

_____

What factors might give a person the strength to refrain from rebelling against God or giving in to fear of people?

_____

_____

_____

_____

_____

Joshua and Caleb were overwhelmingly outnumbered. Panic paralyzed their countrymen. Their ten comrades, all influential leaders among their tribes, dashed icy water over any hope of success. Still Joshua and Caleb refused to back down. They risked death by stoning as they urged the mob to be faithful (Num. 14:10). They knew God would deliver them if only His people would trust Him. Such a stouthearted stand early in Joshua's life offers a glimpse into his character. He held fast to God's word, regardless of the cost. Strong spiritual leadership demands such integrity.

He held fast to God's word, regardless of the cost.

JOSHUA: FAITHFUL IN WORSHIP

"So the LORD spoke to Moses face to face, as a man speaks to his friend. And he would return to the camp, but his servant Joshua the son of Nun, a young man, did not depart from the tabernacle" (Ex. 33:11). The tent of meeting stood off in the distance, representing the place where God encountered His people. When Moses left the camp, heading for the special tabernacle, his short journey always caused a stir in the settlement. Each man would stand in the entrance to his own tent, watching Moses as he disappeared inside the meeting place. As Moses met with God, each man would worship the Lord in the doorway of his own tent (Ex. 33:8–11). When he returned, the radiant glow on Moses' face told everyone he had met with his Lord.

Apparently Moses came and went from God's presence in the tabernacle but Joshua, a young man, remained at the tabernacle. Joshua accompanied Moses to the meeting place but probably did not go inside with Moses. Since the meeting place was a tent, Joshua might have heard God's voice if it was audible. Even if he heard nothing, Joshua would have been aware of the poignancy of those moments. The effect on young Joshua must have been profound. Centuries later, Jesus' conversations with His Father would similarly intrigue His disciples, propelling them to ask how they, too, could meet with God as He did (Luke 11:1).

Joshua apparently chose to spend many hours at the tabernacle. It is God who stirs the hearts of His people to want to draw closer to Him (John 6:44–45, 65). Obviously God was at work in young Joshua's life. Perhaps as Joshua regularly witnessed Moses meeting with God, a growing desire to know God in a similar way swelled within Joshua's heart. Joshua was not content to merely watch others meet with God. He may have dreamed of the day when he would enter the tent as well and meet with God personally. Joshua's tenacity is noteworthy. He stayed longer at the worship site, but his countenance was not changed as Moses' was. The senior leader enjoyed the spiritual intimacy that comes from years of fellowship with God. There are no shortcuts to such a walk. Joshua was still getting to know the Lord, and he wisely seized opportunities to spend time with Him.

PERSONAL RESPONSE

Do you have a growing desire to draw closer to God? How might you act on that desire?

It is God who stirs the hearts of His people who want to grow closer to Him.

_____

_____

_____

While Joshua did everything he could to draw closer to God, God chose to manifest Himself to Joshua and the other Israelites in different ways. Despite Joshua's reverence for God, and despite the fact God spoke often to him, God never caused his face to glow as He did with Moses. This was God's doing. Perhaps God did not want to divide the loyalty of the Israelites between Moses and Joshua.

Sovereign God chose to establish a unique relationship with Moses. Likewise, the Israelites had to remain content with watching from the doorways of their tents as Moses went to meet with God. They had not been summoned into God's presence as Moses had. For them to attempt to force their way into God's presence without a divine invitation would have been lethal (Ex. 19:20–21).

Certainly, Joshua's role as a prominent leader would have given him numerous administrative duties to perform. We do not know all the mundane, time-consuming responsibilities that came with being Moses' right-hand man. Yet Joshua chose to spend every available moment in God's presence. Surely such an investment of time and effort by Joshua as a young man contributed to his lifelong unwavering walk with God. We would do well to emulate his devotion.

ANOTHER LEADER IN GOD'S WORD

ZERUBBABEL: "BY GOD'S SPIRIT"

Zerubbabel, the governor over Jerusalem, oversaw the rebuilding of the temple after the Jewish exiles' return from Babylon. Zerubbabel was confronted with a twofold task: governing a region decimated by war and exile, and rebuilding a massive temple that lay in ruins. As he faced this doubly daunting challenge, he received this message from God: "Not by might nor by power, but by My Spirit,' says the LORD of hosts" (Zech. 4:6).

God was reminding Zerubbabel that spiritual leaders *must* have the Holy Spirit working in their lives even when they are performing what appear to be unspiritual tasks. Zerubbabel faced the tasks of brick and mortar, finances, taxation, and the defeat of enemies, but God reminded him that erecting buildings, administering people, and raising money are all spiritual jobs when the Spirit is involved. Without the Spirit's presence, people may be leaders, but they are not spiritual leaders. Spiritual ends require spiritual means, and spiritual means come only by the Holy Spirit.

In what ways is God speaking to your heart today to recognize that the spiritual goals He has set before you cannot be accomplished apart from the active work of the Holy Spirit in and through your life?

_____

_____

JOSHUA: FAITHFUL TO GOD'S WARNINGS

Joshua's close working relationship with Moses afforded him a good vantage point from which to observe his mentor's faithfulness. It also gave him a unique opportunity to learn from Moses' mistakes. For example, Joshua was present in the wilderness when God told Moses to speak to a rock so water would spring forth for the thirsty Israelites (Num. 20:1–13). But Moses, fed up and angry with his countrymen's murmuring, struck the rock rather than speaking to it as God instructed. Water did gush forth, but God solemnly pronounced: "Because you did not believe Me, to hallow Me in the eyes of the children of Israel, therefore you shall not bring this assembly into the land which I have given them" (Num. 20:12).

God would not tolerate such a display of disobedience even from a spiritual paragon like Moses. Moses' temper cost him immensely. We can only imagine Joshua's shock when Moses gave him the news. Joshua could surely understand why the rebellious Israelites were barred from Canaan. He probably agreed that grumblers like the sons of Korah should be punished for their insolence (Num. 16:1–40). Obviously Aaron, who crafted the golden idol, must suffer the consequences.

But Moses' offense must have seemed minor, especially in light of his faithful track record. Moses had delivered the Israelites from Egypt. He had called down ten plagues on the Egyptians and parted the Red Sea! He had ascended the terrifying Mount Sinai and received God's law. He had spoken with God face-to-face! Surely God would not deny him his heart's desire! Nonetheless, God charged Moses with treating Him irreverently before His followers. And so after forty years of leading God's people, Moses was forced to stop short of his heart's desire.

Imagine the conversations the two leaders shared as they discussed Moses' fate. Did the chagrined mentor urge his protégé to beware of making the same mistake? Did he exhort Joshua to follow God's instructions implicitly, no matter what the circumstances? The lesson for Joshua was clear: walking with God was not about a method; it was about a relationship.

Walking with God was not about a method; it was about a relationship.

Earlier God had instructed Moses to strike a rock, and water had burst forth (Ex. 17:6). The next time the Israelites needed water, God instructed Moses to speak to a rock. Perhaps Moses was too preoccupied with his anger to carefully note the specifics of God's instruction. Perhaps Moses merely resorted to the method that had worked for him the last time (Num. 20:8–12). Whatever the reason, he struck the rock twice instead of speaking to it as he had been instructed. It might seem like hairsplitting, but God knows the heart, and Moses' carelessness cost him dearly.

PERSONAL RESPONSE

Have you ever learned something to *not* do from a mentor? Give a specific example:

_____

_____

_____

How did this impact your own behavior or decision-making?

_____

_____

_____

Obedience, **based on** *faith* **already established, is crucial!**

Both Moses and Joshua knew this wasn't the first time Moses' temper had gotten him in trouble. His choleric outburst against an Egyptian earned him forty years as a fugitive from Egyptian justice (Ex. 2:11–15). Moses' anger would stir him to destroy the original stone tablets upon which the Ten Commandments were written (Ex. 32:19; 34:4). Now his unchecked anger flared up to burn him again. One glance at the forlorn Moses may have turned Joshua's thoughts to the gravity of his own sins.

Joshua was on the receiving end of another golden opportunity—to learn from another's mistakes. To this day God allows people to be publicly and dramatically punished for carelessly disregarding His word. Their humiliation serves as a graphic warning to the rest of us. What a terrifying thing to be an object lesson of God's displeasure (Heb. 10:31)!

Perhaps young Joshua tried to comfort his friend. Perhaps he urged Moses to seek God's reversal of His edict. They both knew Moses had accomplished much in God's service. Surely God would take this into account. Yet, Moses knew God well. He was fully aware of God's holiness. God had every right to command the respect Moses had failed to give Him, and Moses knew it.

God was also sending a stark message to the rest of the people—no one was beyond humble obedience to God. When Moses had plead with God to relent from His judgment, God finally commanded him to never ask again (Deut. 3:23–26). The specter of Moses' situation must have reminded all the people to reflect on their own desperate need to heed God's commands. Obviously *no one* was exempt from accountability to God. This poignant reminder would no doubt serve Joshua well in later years as he took on the role Moses had once held.

Personal Response

What aspect of your personality or nature do you desire God to change?

_____

_____

_____

How might you put yourself in the best position for God to do His life-altering, character-building work?

_____

_____

_____

Joshua: Faithful and Humble Service

Joshua did not weasel and claw his way into anyone's favor. Not God's or man's. Rather, he chose humility and service as his lifestyle. God selected Joshua because of his heart, not because of his political machinations. The Bible repeatedly mentions Joshua's faithfulness to *all* God's commands (Josh. 5:15; 8:35; 10:40; 11:15, 23; 14:5; 23:6; 24:15, 31).

There is no such thing as *partial* obedience. Only total obedience satisfies God's desire for obedience. Like Joshua, we have the choice—either we will serve God with all our heart or we will be disobedient. Joshua learned that God has His own standard for faithfulness, and that makes our own opinions irrelevant. The writer of Proverbs said: "All the ways of a man are pure in his own eyes, but the LORD weighs the spirits" (Prov. 16:2).

Just as partial obedience is an oxymoron; *delayed* obedience is also a contradiction in terms. To put off doing what God commands is a blatant affront to His sovereignty. The moment God spoke, Joshua knew the next thing he did

Just as partial obedience is an oxymoron; *delayed* obedience is also a contradiction in terms.

was crucial. Joshua developed a habit of spontaneous obedience so that when God spoke, Joshua's response was always immediate compliance.

Sometimes Joshua did not know where his obedience would lead him. His ways were not God's ways (Isa. 55:8–9). Nevertheless, he was faithful to God in the small and large assignments. One day he could look back on his life to see a lifelong track record of submission to God.

A faithful life is not built on good intentions, rededications, or New Year's resolutions. It is established on a daily determination to do whatever God says to do. There are no shortcuts to faithfulness. Faithfulness requires a lifetime of daily obedience to the Lord. The accumulation of such obedience defines a mighty servant of God. Joshua became such a person.

CONCEPT REFLECTION

CONCEPT: **There is no such thing as** *partial* **obedience.**

Provide an example of a situation in which you have seen this principle at work:

_____

_____

_____

_____

BIBLE CONTEMPLATION

ISAIAH 55:8–9

"'For My thoughts are not your thoughts, nor are your ways My ways,' says the LORD. 'For as the heavens are higher than the earth, so are My ways higher than your ways, and My thoughts than your thoughts.'"

What does it mean to you that God's thoughts are not your thoughts, and God's ways are not your ways?

_____

_____

_____

What does it mean to you that God's ways and thoughts are higher than yours?

_____

_____

_____

_____

_____

In what ways is trust required in facing the reality that God's ways and thoughts are higher than man's ways and thoughts?

_____

_____

_____

_____

_____

_____

UNIT 3

GOD BUILDS ON THE PAST

> *So Moses arose with his assistant Joshua, and Moses went up to the mountain of God. And he said to the elders, "Wait here for us until we come back to you. Indeed, Aaron and Hur are with you. If any man has a difficulty, let him go to them." Then Moses went up into the mountain, and a cloud covered the mountain.*
>
> ### EXODUS 24:13–15
>
> *So the LORD spoke to Moses face to face, as a man speaks to his friend. And he would return to the camp, but his servant Joshua the son of Nun, a young man, did not depart from the tabernacle.*
>
> ### EXODUS 33:11

Joshua's past served as the foundation for his eventual role as God's statesman. God, not Joshua, set the agenda for Joshua's decisions. God's will, not Joshua's ego, galvanized him to action. As a result, every event in Joshua's life became a building block in the magnificent life God was creating.

Joshua's life was not dependent on random chance or the exertion of human will. His was a purposeful life that brought glory to God. Joshua was not a prisoner of his past; he overcame his upbringing and allowed God to build a bright future for him.

Joshua's past became the foundation for his eventual role as God's statesman.

DAY ONE

THE IMPACT OF THE PAST

How does our past affect our leadership ability? For example, some people grew up in dysfunctional homes devoid of parental nurture. As a result, they lack self-confidence and certain people skills essential for strong leadership. Has their past precluded them from any hope of leading in the future?

People face many questions as God develops them as leaders. Is the way we follow today important in determining whether or not we lead tomorrow? Also, are all people called to lead at some level? Is the reason certain people always remain in an assistant's role because they stopped allowing God to develop them into the leaders they could have become if they had only yielded to His will? Or, is it a legitimate calling to be an assistant all your life?

How do we follow a great leader? How do we build upon what has gone before us?

What difference does the Holy Spirit make in our leadership? Can the Spirit make anyone into a leader? How is the working of the Holy Spirit in our lives a prerequisite for God's future assignments for us?

How do leaders cope with change? The organization as they first knew it may have changed significantly. The circumstances in which they work may be in flux. How do leaders continue to lead their people forward when those things they counted on in the past are no longer a reality? These are the practical issues today's leaders must address. Studying how Joshua dealt with them will shed light on our circumstances as well.

At least two types of history exercise a significant influence upon people. The first is that over which you have no control: the nationality of your birth, your family's socioeconomic status, the presence or absence of a nurturing atmosphere in your home, and so on.

Likewise, the history of the organization you lead is something you inherit: the church you serve was torn by a split five years before you arrived as pastor; your predecessor in the company embezzled funds from the business, and now you work under a cloud of suspicion. This history occurred completely apart from you but now bears its weight upon you.

PERSONAL RESPONSE

Think of the factors related to your life and work over which you have *no* personal control, such as your nationality, socioeconomic factors, parental influences, and structure of the organization in which you work. List the *no control* factors:

_____

_____

_____

Write several words describing the factors most pertinent to your life today:

_____

_____

_____

Another Leader in God's Word

Your Place in Your Organization's History

God does not work in a vacuum. He has been unfolding His plan since the beginning of time, including His plan for the organization you are leading. Leaders are remiss if they make decisions as if there were no track record or history related to their organization. Spiritual leaders, especially, should recognize with an even greater sense of accountability that God has led them to their organization to fulfill a particular part of His greater plan in this particular time.

Isaac knew the same God who led him had also led his father, Abraham (Gen. 26:24).

Joseph knew that God's activity in his life was building on what God had already done through his ancestors Abraham, Isaac, and Jacob (Gen. 48:15).

Moses knew that God was using him to implement a plan that had been in place long before Moses' time (Ex. 3:15).

When Paul preached before those who were "hearing his case," he reviewed the story of how God had worked in his life over time (Acts 22:1–21, 24; 24:10–21; 26:1–23).

Esther was brought to a keen awareness that God had placed her in a specific place and time for a specific purpose. Her relative Mordecai said to her, "Yet who knows whether you have come to the kingdom for such a time as this?" (Est. 4:14).

In what ways do you recognize that God has prepared a group of people "for such a time as this"?

_____

_____

_____

In what ways do you recognize that God has prepared *you* to lead your organization at this particular time in history?

_____

_____

_____

> **God does not work in a vacuum. He has been unfolding His plan since the beginning of time, including His plan for the organization you are leading.**

A second type of history is your own personal background. The way you conducted your life as a young person can directly impact your later adult life. The diligence with which you pursued your education or your first jobs can exact long-lasting consequences. This is the more recent history in your life, and it includes events and attitudes over which you exercised some control. You are now facing the consequences for an accumulation of decisions you made in earlier years.

PERSONAL RESPONSE

What are some recent events or experiences over which you have had personal control?

_____

_____

_____

Identify your attitude, behavior, and the resulting consequences:

EVENT	ATTITUDE	BEHAVIOR	CONSEQUENCES
_____	_____	_____	_____
_____	_____	_____	_____
_____	_____	_____	_____
_____	_____	_____	_____
_____	_____	_____	_____
_____	_____	_____	_____
_____	_____	_____	_____
_____	_____	_____	_____
_____	_____	_____	_____

Both Joshua's national history and his personal history profoundly affected the role he played as a spiritual leader. Every day Joshua faced the consequences of mistakes others had committed. He also reaped the benefits of the wise decisions he had made in his past. The following pages consider some of the significant ways history intersected Joshua's life.

DAY TWO

JOSHUA WAS FIRST A GOOD ASSISTANT

One of the main reasons Joshua became such a successful leader was because he first was a faithful and conscientious assistant.

There is no such thing as a born leader. Becoming a good leader is a process. When God prepares someone for a significant assignment, He is thorough and systematic. His pattern, as revealed in the Scriptures, is to build character and leadership skills step by step. When people prove faithful in small assignments, they are given larger ones (Matt. 25:21, 23).

Generally when God wants to develop leaders He begins by teaching them how to be good followers. However, not everyone is comfortable with secondary positions. Often aspiring leaders chafe under their subordinate roles in their impatience to take charge. But both biblical and secular histories relate numerous examples of successful leaders who first proved themselves faithful followers.

Jacob's son Joseph seemed to know this instinctively as he faithfully served Potiphar and the Egyptian jailor before reaching the apex of power under the pharaoh. Conversely, the disciple Peter had to go against his impulsive, outspoken nature to learn this truth.

> **There is no such thing as a born leader. Becoming a good leader is a process.**

BIBLE CONTEMPLATION

> ### MATTHEW 25:23
> *"His lord said to him, 'Well done, good and faithful servant; you have been faithful over a few things, I will make you ruler over many things. Enter into the joy of your lord.'"*

Cite an example in which you have seen this principle in action. Have you personally been called a "good and faithful servant" in a small matter, with a subsequent promotion?

_____

_____

_____

_____

_____

Joshua had the mettle required to serve as a capable assistant before taking over command himself. Moses was not the easiest person to assist. He was poor at delegation (Ex. 18:13–27). He could not always handle those with opposing opinions (Num. 13:28–14:5). He was susceptible to outbursts of anger (Ex. 2:11–12; 32:19; Num. 20:10–11). Nonetheless, there is no record of Joshua complaining about Moses. On the contrary, he repeatedly defended his leader's honor and reputation.

PERSONAL RESPONSE

Do you find it difficult to defend a leader's position of authority when that leader exhibits flaws? Why?

_____

_____

_____

What approach or strategy do you employ?

_____

_____

_____

While he served as Moses' assistant, Joshua was protective of his leader's position and authority among the people. When Eldad and Medad began prophesying in the camp, Joshua saw this as a challenge to Moses' leadership, so he urged Moses to stop them (Num. 11:28).

But Moses, with characteristic humility, gently and wisely responded, "Are you zealous for my sake? Oh, that all the LORD's people were prophets and that the LORD would put His Spirit upon them!" (Num. 11:29). Joshua never sided with Moses' critics, of whom there were many. Rather, Joshua's loyalty lay with his leader, and he would support him even in the face of widespread unpopularity.

Joshua never appeared concerned with building his own reputation or gaining recognition for his own accomplishments. He simply served to the best of his ability wherever God placed him. It was God who determined how and when Joshua was promoted as a leader, and it was God who ultimately chose to make Joshua one of the most successful and famous generals in his nation's history.

CONCEPT REFLECTION

CONCEPT: Joshua never appeared concerned about building his own reputation or gaining recognition for his own accomplishments.

Do you find it difficult to take this stance when the culture proclaims so insistently: "promote yourself—look out for number one"? Why?

_____

_____

_____

> Joshua never appeared concerned about building his own reputation or gaining recognition for his own accomplishments.

What strategy or approach do you take?

_____

_____

_____

The difference between the top position and the second in command can be enormous. While there can be far more prestige and recognition coming to the former, there are also burdens they carry that no one else can share. Joshua would have certainly seen some advantages to remaining second in command.

Leading an entire nation, especially one as recalcitrant as Israel, would have been an onerous burden to assume. People lined up for hours to speak with Moses, not Joshua. Malcontents castigated Moses, not Joshua. Joshua saw firsthand how unappreciated Moses often was for his efforts.

Joshua could have settled into a comfortable position in middle management and closed the door to what God had in mind for him. Joshua could have ended his days as Moses' assistant and history would have granted him minor mention in the scriptural record, but he would have robbed himself and his country of the mighty work God intended to do through his life.

PERSONAL RESPONSE

Recall a situation in which you were an assistant to a leader. How did you handle that role?

_____

_____

_____

What might you do differently if you had it to do over again?

_____

_____

_____

ANOTHER LEADER IN GOD'S WORD

JESUS: BOTH LEADER AND FOLLOWER

Jesus is our most compelling model of good leadership. His leadership style, however, is not rooted in methodology, but rather His relationship with the Father and His absolute obedience to the Father's will. Jesus is not only the consummate spiritual leader, but also the consummate spiritual follower. God does not ask leaders to dream big dreams for Him or to solve problems that confront them. He asks leaders to walk with Him so intimately that when He reveals what is on His agenda, they will immediately adjust their lives to His will and the results will bring glory to God.

What challenges have you experienced in following God as you lead people?

_____

_____

_____

_____

How can a person prevent their own agenda and dream from making them unable to discern or yield to God's agenda?

_____

_____

_____

_____

DAY THREE

EVALUATING THE ROLE OF AN ASSISTANT

Would Joshua have been just as successful had he always remained Moses' assistant? Can the role of assistant be a legitimate calling in itself or is it merely a step in God's preparation process for a higher leadership position? If people are continually growing and developing in their leadership skills, will they not eventually be prepared to assume a senior leadership role? These are questions those in secondary leadership roles must ask.

PERSONAL RESPONSE

Identify one role (for example: at work, in a church, in a club) in which you may be middle management—not on the bottom rung of the organizational ladder but not at the top: _____

Do you regard this position as permanent or preparatory? _____

How do you feel about the possibility God might see your position differently?

_____

_____

_____

Not everyone who serves in middle management is necessarily called to upper management. Their position in their organization does not reflect whether or not God is working in their life. Personal and professional development can and does take place at any level of an organization. Leadership is not performed exclusively at the top of the organizational chart.

We know numerous associate pastors and middle managers who are at the center of all that is happening in their organizations. One does not have to spend much time around them to recognize God is using them powerfully in the roles to which He has called them. They experience challenges and contentment where they are, and they do not require promotions to be effective.

The key to one's leadership position rests with God. God assigns some people to work as assistants to other leaders. God calls others into roles as senior leaders.

The key is not our aspirations or our ego needs or our insecurities. The key is God's assignment. Those coveting positions of top leadership may not possess the character to hold such a position. On the other hand, some people avoiding leadership positions may be running from God's will. Every one of us must stand before God and ask what God is calling us to do, regardless of our preferences.

Many talented people avoid leadership positions like the plague! Others do not feel called by God to lead. Some are fearful to lead. Many suffer insecurities that convince them they cannot lead. Some recognize that to lead would require the investment of far more effort than they are willing to make. Others possess a profound sense of humility that prefers to support others who are in the forefront. Not everyone is attracted to top leadership positions. Those who believe a supportive role is their calling can learn at least three significant lessons from Joshua.

> **The key is not our aspirations or our ego needs or our insecurities. The key is God's assignment.**

PERSONAL RESPONSE

Have you ever found yourself shying away from a leadership position? Why?

_____

_____

_____

Added Insight into Spiritual Leadership

Leader or Manager?

There's a difference between leaders and managers. Managers often become embroiled in the daily grind . . . leaders step back from day-to-day operations to gain perspective on broader issues related to their organization.

Managers feel responsible for *how* something is done . . . leaders must also consider *why* it is being done and communicate this to their followers.

Managers oversee and supervise processes related to the pursuit of goals . . . leaders oversee and supervise the establishment of an organization's direction and goals.

Are you a manager or a leader? _____ How so?

_____

_____

_____

Joshua sought to grow personally in whatever position God assigned to him.

LESSON 1: Joshua always sought to grow personally in whatever position God assigned to him. He didn't confine himself to his own comfort level. He grew personally and professionally throughout his life. Each step of faith was foundational for greater accomplishments God purposed to complete through him. Not all of God's greater assignments for Joshua resulted in a promotion or a new leadership position. But every new challenge revealed a little more to Joshua about who God is. It is often through crises that a leader experiences the deepest dimensions of God's love and power. God is always seeking to work in the lives of His servants to increase their trust in Him (Matt. 25:14–30; Luke 19:17).

Concept Reflection

CONCEPT: God is always seeking to work in the lives of His servants to increase their trust in Him.

In what ways has a challenge or crisis impacted the way you trust the Lord?

_____

_____

_____

Forty years is a long time to wait for a promotion. But for Joshua, those four decades were anything but stagnant. He walked through numerous diverse and multifaceted challenges during his time in the desert. God taught Joshua that the key to people's success is not the rung they reach on the corporate ladder but the level of intimacy they reach with God. Whether Joshua was experiencing prosperity in the promised land or suffering exile in the wilderness, he could still enjoy a close relationship with almighty God.

The position Joshua held had nothing to do with his accessibility to God. When Joshua's lengthy stint as Moses' assistant drew to a close, he emerged fully prepared to lead because of all God had been doing in his life. When Joshua became the senior leader of the Israelites, it was not to escape the monotony or emptiness of his role as an assistant; it was a natural step in the process of walking with God year by year.

That being said, whether it is short term or long term, the job of assistant requires a clear sense of calling. Joshua knew he was called to an associate's role. Whether or not God ever adjusted that role was up to God. Joshua's responsibility was to serve. Likewise, a person ought to remain in his secondary leadership role for as long as he continues to feel a specific calling to it.

LESSON 2: Christians who experience success as assistants keep their focus on the kingdom of God rather than on their careers. We've known many people who were so active in their local churches that they bypassed promotions and transfers in their jobs, along with the accompanying salaries and prestige. They did so because the new role would have hindered them from serving the Lord in the same manner they were accustomed to in their current positions.

Some businesspeople, knowing they were called first to be leaders in their own homes, have declined promotions because the increased responsibilities would create undue hardships on their families. Such people clearly understand the difference between their vocation and their calling. Whereas they must have a vocation to earn a living, their calling is to bring glory to God. God's assignments do not always coincide with career advancement.

CONCEPT REFLECTION

CONCEPT: **God's assignments do not always coincide with career advancement.**

How do you personally determine if God is calling you to remain in a position or to accept a promotion or advancement?

God's assignments do not always coincide with career advancement.

_____

_____

How difficult would it be for you to turn down the offer of a promotion or advancement?

_____

_____

_____

What are some reasons it might be difficult to accept a promotion or advancement?

_____

_____

_____

LESSON 3: Joshua modeled a deep-rooted humility. There is no evidence Joshua struggled with ego. He never made demands on Moses or the people for recognition of his service. He did not submit a résumé for the position Moses was vacating. He wholly trusted his career into the sovereign hands of God.

Humble people like Joshua find joy in serving and do not need the limelight to find contentment. These people derive pleasure from making others successful. History's great leaders have invariably been surrounded by such people. Few, if any, outstanding leaders achieve success without the dedicated service of capable associates.

A caution is in order here. While God calls some people to invest themselves in supportive roles all their lives, others grasp these positions in default of what God intended for them. Associates who remain in their roles because they are unwilling to assume more responsibility will never experience the same level of fulfillment as people who are associates because that is exactly where God called them to be.

Again, the key is God's will. Every Christian would do well to learn from Joshua's example. He was content in his role as associate, but he was also willing to take on the role of primary leader if God told him to do so. Spiritual leaders maintain an obedient attitude. They find fulfillment in whatever role God assigns them, but this does not mean they close themselves off to whatever new direction God has for them. If you are currently in an associate position, it's crucial for you to clarify whether you are there at God's invitation or at your own hesitation.

> **Few, if any, outstanding leaders achieve success without the dedicated service of capable associates.**

ADDED INSIGHT INTO
SPIRITUAL LEADERSHIP

SOURCES OF INFLUENCE

Influence can come from a variety of sources, some legitimate and others questionable. Influence in itself is not evidence of true leadership if that influence is gained improperly. Here are three *illegitimate* ways people gain influence over others:

1. Position—being promoted to a supervisory or assuming a managerial position

2. Power—including political force, the use of weapons or money, and any other attempt to control others

3. Personality—popularity, charisma, charm

Here are five *legitimate* sources of influence:

1. God's Authentication—an affirmation by God of a person's position and calling.

2. Encounters with God—the leader has unique, profound, life-changing encounters with God that require the leader's total submission to God and result in the leader's being more yielded in faith to trust God and do His will.

3. Character/Integrity—spiritual leaders must be recognized for their honesty, integrity, morality . . . they must "be diligent to be found by Him in peace, without spot and blameless" (2 Peter 3:14).

4. A Successful Track Record—a pattern of faithfulness and obedience in every assignment God gives them, producing spiritual growth and respect from others that is earned, not demanded.

5. Preparation—spiritual leaders must train, take time to learn, and prepare for the demands of their God-given assignments.

As you have read through these legitimate and illegitimate sources of influence, which one stood out to you? _____

What do you believe God may be speaking to you about the source of the influence you are exerting on your followers?

_____

_____

_____

JOSHUA SUCCEEDED A GREAT LEADER

Replacing a successful leader is a good thing. But stepping into the shoes of a great leader may put the newcomer at a distinct disadvantage. The issue is expectations. Those accustomed to highly effective leadership expect nothing less from the successor. Leadership styles differ, and most people can eventually adjust to that, but there are higher expectations when the predecessor sets the bar high. This can certainly intimidate novice leaders who have not yet reached their full potential. How would you like to have followed the man Joshua succeeded? Scripture describes Moses at the end of his life this way:

> But since then there has not arisen in Israel a prophet like Moses, whom the LORD knew face to face, in all the signs and wonders which the LORD sent him to do in the land of Egypt, before Pharaoh, before all his servants, and in all his land, and by all that mighty power and all the great terror which Moses performed in the sight of all Israel. (Deuteronomy 34:10–12)

There could be no questioning Moses' stellar track record. He set an incredibly high standard. When a sea blocked the way, Moses parted it! When his countrymen were hungry, he showered them with manna and quail from the sky! When they were thirsty, he called forth water from a rock! After he spoke with God, his face took on a supernatural glow! Those who criticized him contracted leprosy (Num. 12:1–16)! Those who opposed him saw the earth open up to swallow them in its depths! God poured out His power through Moses' life in an unprecedented way. Now Moses was gone, and the people looked to Joshua to see what kind of leader *he* would be.

Throughout the book of Joshua, Moses is called "the servant of the LORD" (Josh. 1:1; 8:31; 9:24; 12:6). Joshua, on the other hand, is described as "Moses' servant" (Ex. 24:13; 33:11; Num. 11:28; Josh. 1:1). The Bible does not call Joshua the "servant of the LORD" until his death (Josh. 24:29; Judg. 2:8). What was it like for Joshua to be known as "the servant of Moses"? After all, Joshua was a mighty warrior in his own right. He had been faithful to God in all things, even more so than Moses had been. It may have seemed that Joshua would always remain eclipsed in Moses' shadow.

PERSONAL RESPONSE

How hard is it for you to be in a secondary role?

_____

_____

_____

What kind of follower are you?

_____

_____

_____

You can tell a lot about leaders by watching how they handle the ghosts of their predecessors. The greatest obstacle in effectively succeeding an esteemed leader is the hurdle of pride. Joshua did not seem to resent following the mighty Moses, though he must have felt daunted by the task. Perhaps that's why, when Joshua first assumed command, God repeatedly encouraged him not to be afraid but to be courageous (Josh. 1:6–7, 9).

Joshua accepted Moses' work as foundational to his own rather than as a threat to his success. Joshua did not have to dismantle or criticize Moses' accomplishments in order to elevate himself; instead he chose to build upon the foundation Moses had laid. That is why God honored him. Joshua honored God by honoring what God had done through Moses.

You can tell a lot about leaders by watching how they handle the ghosts of their predecessors.

The greatest obstacle in effectively succeeding an esteemed leader is the hurdle of pride.

PERSONAL RESPONSE

What difficulties have you faced in building upon a foundation laid by someone before you (for example: at work, in your family heritage, in a church, in a club)?

_____

_____

_____

_____

_____

The same situation was later mirrored in the relationship between the prophet Elijah and his protégé, Elisha. Elijah was one of the greatest prophets in history. He prayed and the rain stopped falling for three years. His prayers also brought fire descending from heaven to consume his sacrifice, altar and all (1 Kings 18:20–46). What an intimidating leader to replace!

When Elisha learned he would be Elijah's successor, he asked for and received a double portion of the Spirit that inhabited Elijah. Elisha knew it was God's Spirit who empowered Elijah, and the same Spirit would have to strengthen him if he were to follow such a famous prophet.

Bible scholars identify eight miracles performed by Elijah and sixteen by Elisha. Elisha didn't resent God's activity in his predecessor's life. Neither did he feel threatened by Elijah's illustrious career. He learned from it. He wisely concluded if God's Spirit worked so powerfully through Elijah, the same Spirit could empower him for a dynamic ministry as well.

The apostle Paul addressed this issue with the church at Corinth. Some of the Corinthian believers had been deeply affected by Apollos's ministry. Others were staunchly loyal to Paul. To Paul's dismay, the church was dividing according to which spiritual leader held their allegiance. Paul clarified: "I planted, Apollos watered, but God gave the increase" (1 Cor. 3:6).

God's servants come and go, but God is the One who accomplishes the work. Spiritual leaders have a role to play, but they are instruments in God's hand. Leaders are wise to remember that long after they leave their organizations, God will remain. And, as long as they are in their leadership positions, they are God's servants. Pride has no place in service to God.

PERSONAL RESPONSE

What difficulties have you faced in remaining humble in the wake of your own successes?

_____

_____

_____

_____

_____

What can a leader do to effectively and sincerely give God all the glory when people are offering their applause and congratulatory remarks?

_____

_____

_____

_____

JOSHUA'S PAST PREPARED HIM
FOR THE FUTURE

Joshua did not become a person of integrity *after* his appointment as leader. His integrity preceded and led to his assignment. Did Joshua become a man of God the moment Moses laid hands on him? No. The Bible reveals that when Moses commissioned him, Joshua was already filled with the Holy Spirit: "And the LORD said to Moses: 'Take Joshua the son of Nun with you, a man in whom is the Spirit, and lay your hand on him; set him before Eleazar the priest and before all the congregation, and inaugurate him in their sight'" (Num. 27:18–19).

Moses apparently laid his hands on Joshua because the Spirit was *already* working powerfully in Joshua. How did Moses know who his successor would be? God showed him the man in whom His Spirit had already been powerfully working. Moses simply affirmed the Holy Spirit's presence in Joshua's life.

Faithfulness comes from your character, not from your title.

CONCEPT REFLECTION

CONCEPT: **Faithfulness comes from your character, not from your title.**

Cite an example in which a person's *lack* of faithfulness or integrity disqualified him or her from a promotion or position:

_____

_____

_____

What happened later to the person?

_____

_____

_____

Can you picture God saying, "Lay your hands on Joshua, and when he realizes I have called him, he will get more serious about his faith"? Joshua already *was* a Spirit-filled man of God. That is why God chose him for such a significant assignment.

**Faithfulness comes
from your character,
not from your title.**

Joshua did not become a person of integrity *after* his appointment as leader. His integrity preceded and led to his assignment.

Those who hold a position of spiritual leadership without experiencing the active working of the Holy Spirit are courting humiliating failure.

During Old Testament times, God gave people tasks and then enabled them to accomplish their assignments by placing the Holy Spirit in their lives. For example, God called Bezalel to construct the tabernacle and then "filled him with the Spirit of God, in wisdom, in understanding, in knowledge, and in all manner of workmanship" (Ex. 31:1–3). God commissioned Samson as a deliverer for His people and then placed His Spirit on him to give him unusual strength (Judg. 14:19; 15:14). In Joshua's case the gift of the Spirit came *before* the assignment, a truly unusual occurrence for the Old Testament era.

Joshua's new assignment was a natural outflow of what God had already been doing in his life. God did not begin working in Joshua's life once he became a leader. Rather, Joshua became the leader *because* God had already been working in his life. Your relationship with God is far more important than any position. Those who hold a position of spiritual leadership without experiencing the active working of the Holy Spirit are courting humiliating failure.

If you are a spiritual leader, or if you want to become one, the most important thing you can do is to concentrate on your walk with God. If the Holy Spirit is actively involved in your life, guiding your decisions and empowering your actions, then your life will exert a tremendous influence on others.

PERSONAL RESPONSE

What could you do today to intentionally concentrate more on your walk with God? Be specific:

_____

_____

_____

What could you do to allow the Holy Spirit to be more actively involved in your life—guiding your decisions and empowering your actions? Be specific:

_____

_____

_____

When Joshua took over from Moses, he inherited some logistical headaches. One of his most pressing concerns was how to feed the vast multitude under his care. Moses had committed his grievous sin while attempting to provide water for the vast crowd (Num. 20:1–13). For forty years the Israelites had gathered manna every morning to feed their families for that day. It was like a light frost on the ground that tasted like milk and honey (Ex. 16:14, 31). Thus they were reminded daily of what they were missing in the promised land. It was only a faint taste of what they would have enjoyed in abundance had they obeyed God.

Then an interesting thing happened once Joshua led the Israelites across the Jordan River into the promised land. The manna that had routinely fallen from heaven for forty years suddenly stopped (Josh. 5:12). Manna was all the young Israelites knew. They had been gathering it each morning for their entire lives. It met their needs nutritionally, but they had never tasted "real" food. Then suddenly the manna ceased.

Now that they were in the luxuriant promised land, the Israelites needn't continue their subsistence lifestyle. God wanted them to enjoy the bounty He had provided them, even if it meant taking it away from giants in walled cities! This posed a problem for Joshua. Food no longer fell from the sky; now they had to fight for it. Moses had his concerns in the wilderness and now, in the promised land, Joshua had his own unique challenges.

PERSONAL RESPONSE

What challenges do you face today that your predecessor never encountered?

_____

_____

_____

_____

How are you responding to those challenges?

_____

_____

_____

_____

> **Leaders do not choose the time in which they lead.**

> **Leaders do not complain about the unique challenges facing them. True leaders tackle challenges and, with God's help, overcome them.**

Leaders do not choose the time in which they lead. Some serve in periods of prosperity and peace. Others come to the helm just as their ship enters turbulent waters.

Sometimes, adversity actually propels leaders to greatness by drawing on the deep reserves of their character. Leaders do not complain about the unique challenges facing them. True leaders tackle challenges and, with God's help, overcome them.

PERSONAL RESPONSE

To what degree are you comfortable with change?

_____

_____

_____

If you are uncomfortable with change, how could you become more comfortable?

_____

_____

_____

Some people struggle with change. They like to nestle into an organization and keep everything the way it is. Yet change is occurring today at a dizzying pace. Those who get lost in the sentimental memories of yesterday will be of no use to organizations today.

Modern leaders accept change, whether good or bad, as a matter of course. Rather than resisting change, they capitalize on it. Rather than grieving over what has been lost, they grow excited about what can happen. Astute leaders embrace the reality of inevitable change, and they seek ways God will use them to make a significant difference in the midst of it.

Joshua had the privilege of leading his people into a lush and fertile land. But along with this opportunity came a completely new set of demands. Whereas Moses hadn't had to concern himself with feeding his people for forty years, Joshua was going to face this enormous challenge daily. It was a significant additional burden for Joshua.

However, rather than bemoaning this fact, Joshua faced the future boldly, based on his observations from the past. The lesson Joshua learned while serving under Moses was not that God provided _manna_ but that God _provided_. God had sustained the Israelites for forty years, even while they were disobedient. Surely they could trust God's care as they obeyed Him in the present.

Joshua did not expect God to work in exactly the same ways He had during Moses' tenure. He simply trusted God's sovereignty and counted on Him to act in a way that demonstrated His love for them. The Bible doesn't indicate that the Israelites ever lacked food or water while they followed Joshua. Had God continued to send manna in the same old way, the people would have missed out on the feast God had prepared for them in the promised land.

> **The lesson Joshua learned while serving under Moses was not that God provided _manna_ but that God _provided_.**

UNIT 3—GOD BUILDS ON THE PAST

ALLOWING GOD TO WORK

Joshua's difficult beginnings could have crippled him with insecurities. But Joshua didn't focus on his past, except to learn from it. He allowed God to create something unique with his life. Joshua trusted God to guide him through each new situation.

As Moses' assistant, Joshua was diligent and patient. He allowed God to work thoroughly in his life. Joshua didn't campaign for a prominent position among the Israelites. He simply served God and trusted Him. God is the One who chose Joshua and fashioned him into an effective and respected leader.

Now it's time for some honest self-evaluation. First, consider the type of follower you are. Everyone is accountable to someone. Are you loyal? Dependable? Are you the type of follower you would like to have serving under you?

Second, consider what type of leader you are. Are you a dynamic person who is always learning and growing? Or, have you settled into an attitude of complacency? Leaders, of all people, can never afford to stop growing.

If God has been stretching you through your circumstances, how are you facing the challenge? Could He be preparing you for a new role? What do you value more—your relationship with God or your position with people?

PERSONAL RESPONSE

Are you truly willing to allow God to work in your life, or do you feel compelled to make things happen?

_____

_____

What kind of follower are you? Describe your style as a follower:

_____

_____

_____

_____

What type of leader are you? Describe your leadership style:

_____

_____

_____

_____

Are you learning and growing, or complacent and resistant to change?

_____

_____

_____

ANOTHER LEADER IN GOD'S WORD

MOSES: ADEPT AT DELEGATING

Moses' stature as a national leader among his people was unparalleled. Everyone knew Moses spoke face-to-face with God. Whenever a dispute arose, people naturally wanted Moses to settle the matter. The result? Long lines of people waited their turn with him (Ex. 18:13–26). From morning until night, Moses dealt with issues that others could have processed for him. Jethro, Moses' father-in-law, finally intervened. He instructed Moses about how to delegate responsibility so that Moses handled only the most difficult cases and allowed others to decide routine issues. Not only was Moses' administrative load greatly relieved, but the people received answers and justice in a prompter and more efficient manner.

Many leaders make the assumption, as Moses perhaps did, that because they are able to do something, they should do something. Other leaders make the mistake of assuming that they alone are capable of managing or deciding all details. Still others believe if they don't micromanage their organizations, they will lose prestige or control. The result, however, of a leader doing it all is greater stress not only for the leader but also for the entire organization.

A leader needs to ask continually, "Is this something someone else could do?"

Is there something you are doing today that somebody else *could* do?

_____

_____

_____

_____

UNIT 4

GOD'S PRESENCE:
THE SECRET TO SUCCESS

> *After the death of Moses the servant of the LORD, it came to pass that the LORD spoke to Joshua the son of Nun, Moses' assistant, saying: "Moses My servant is dead. Now therefore, arise, go over this Jordan, you and all this people, to the land which I am giving to them—the children of Israel. Every place that the sole of your foot will tread upon I have given you, as I said to Moses. From the wilderness and this Lebanon as far as the great river, the River Euphrates, all the land of the Hittites, and to the Great Sea toward the going down of the sun, shall be your territory. No man shall be able to stand before you all the days of your life; as I was with Moses, so I will be with you. I will not leave you nor forsake you."*
>
> ## JOSHUA 1:1–5

The difference the Holy Spirit makes in a life is astronomical. No one, no matter how creative or talented, can duplicate or manufacture what the Spirit can do in the life of someone yielded to God.

Joshua was a skilled military leader but his success came from his walk with God, not from his military prowess. He needed more than strategic planning to accomplish God's purposes. He needed God. This chapter will examine some of the ways God's presence made a pronounced difference in Joshua's leading.

DAY ONE

JOSHUA EXERCISED GOOD LEADERSHIP

Clearly Joshua's success was rooted in his dependence on God. Yet Joshua also modeled good leadership principles as he led the Israelites. For example, Joshua

He needed more than strategic planning to accomplish God's purposes. He needed God.

knew how to act quickly. The ability and willingness to take decisive and timely action can mean the difference between victory and defeat. Joshua used the rapid advance of his army to throw his enemies off balance.

When Israel's allies, the Gibeonites, were suddenly besieged by five Amorite kings, it appeared the Amorites could easily overwhelm the vastly outnumbered Gibeonites (Josh. 10:5–9). Joshua responded immediately and marched his men from Gilgal through the night. The Israelites surprised the Amorites the following morning, catching them off guard and winning a spectacular victory.

CONCEPT REFLECTION

CONCEPT: **The ability and willingness to take decisive and timely action can mean the difference between victory and defeat.**

Can you provide a personal example in which *decisive* or *timely* action was critical to victory?

_____

_____

_____

Can you provide a personal example in which *indecisive* or *untimely* action resulted in defeat?

_____

_____

_____

Joshua worked closely with his key leaders. The elders of Israel apparently respected him. Unlike Moses, who tended at times to work alone, Joshua was a team player (Ex. 2:11–12; 18; 33:7). Joshua was secure in his walk with God. He never acted intimidated or threatened by other influential leaders. The people did not complain or rebel against his leadership. In fact, they continued to follow his instructions even after his death until their generation passed from the scene (Judg. 2:7).

PERSONAL RESPONSE

From your perspective, what attributes are necessary to be a team player?

_____

_____

_____

Modern leadership gurus regularly advocate servant leadership as the preeminent way to influence others. In that regard, Joshua was centuries ahead of his time. He refused to set himself above the hardships his people experienced. He was God's servant, not the people's king, and that reality dramatically influenced the way he led people. When he set an ambush for the people of Ai, he personally took the place of greatest peril. He intentionally occupied the most dangerous position on the battlefield (Josh. 8:4–22).

Joshua could have hidden in ambush with twenty-five thousand men; instead he stationed himself among the five thousand soldiers who staged a difficult retreat so the enemy would chase after them and abandon the protection of their city. Such courageous leadership did not go unnoticed among his men. Soldiers are much more motivated to follow a leader who never asks them to do anything he is not willing to do himself.

PERSONAL RESPONSE

How do you feel when a leader indulges in special privileges?

_____

_____

_____

How do you feel when a leader refuses to accept or indulge in special privileges?

_____

_____

_____

Some of history's most famous military leaders refused to order their people to do something they, themselves, were unwilling to do.

A highly respected leader himself, Joshua did not use his prominent position for selfish purposes. After having faithfully led the Israelites to a brilliant conquest of Canaan, we do not find Joshua ever making demands of his people as a reward for his services. We never hear of an exalted title or extravagant wealth that came to Joshua as a prize for his success.

We never see Joshua demanding respect from his people. There are no accusations of mismanagement of funds or of abuse of power. The Israelites believed Joshua was leading in order to bring glory to God and to bless the people of God. Such leadership inspired a loyal following. Jesus explained this leadership approach:

> You know that the rulers of the Gentiles lord it over them, and those who are great exercise authority over them. Yet it shall not be so among you; but who-

ever desires to become great among you, let him be your servant. And whoever desires to be first among you, let him be your slave—just as the Son of Man did not come to be served, but to serve, and to give His life a ransom for many. (Matthew 20:25–28)

PERSONAL RESPONSE

How do you feel when a highly respected or successful leader becomes wealthy or has been able to broker a prominent position, partly because of the work you did for that person?

_____

_____

_____

To what extent do you believe a leader deserves or should receive rewards that come *after* a position of active leadership (for example, rewards to a retired war hero)?

_____

_____

_____

How do you feel when a leader *demands* respect?

_____

_____

_____

How do you feel when a leader abuses power or mishandles funds?

_____

_____

_____

Reflect upon your answers to the questions above. What qualities do you hold to be important for a godly leader when it comes to personal reward?

_____

_____

_____

Joshua can take his rightful place as a fearless military leader in his own right. He seems to have been a natural leader in many respects. Yet Joshua had something these other leaders lacked: he had God's presence. Joshua led a defeated, ragtag group of former slaves to seemingly impossible victories. That took more than good leadership; it took *God's* leadership.

ANOTHER LEADER IN GOD'S WORD

DEBORAH: GOD'S ABIDING PRESENCE

Deborah served as a judge of God's people during a dangerous and turbulent period in Israel's history. People came to her from far away to hear her judgments and words of wisdom. She was not trained in military tactics, nor was she a valiant warrior, but Barak, the commander of Israel's army, came to receive Deborah's counsel from God. She told him that God would give his forces victory over their oppressors. Despite this assurance, Barak recognized God's dynamic presence in Deborah's life and said to her, "If you will go with me, then I will go; but if you will not go with me, I will not go" (Judg. 4:8).

When people come to you for counsel, do you rely on your own wisdom or God's wisdom? _____ Do those who come to you for counsel recognize God's presence at work in your life? _____ How so?

_____

_____

_____

DAY TWO

JOSHUA RECEIVED GOD'S AFFIRMATION

Joshua inherited a monumental assignment from Moses. He was expected to succeed where his mentor had failed. He knew the people had grumbled against Moses for forty years; he probably expected his stubborn countrymen to resist his leadership as well. God's words must have brought tremendous relief to Joshua as he prepared to lead the Israelites. This is what the Lord told him:

No man shall be able to stand before you all the days of your life; as I was with Moses, so I will be with you. I will not leave you nor forsake you. Be strong and of good courage, for to this people you shall divide as an inheritance the land which I swore to their fathers to give them. Only be strong and very courageous, that you may observe to do according to all the law which Moses My servant commanded you; do not turn from it to the right hand or to the left, that you may prosper wherever you go. This Book of the Law shall not depart from your mouth, but you shall meditate in it day and night, that you may observe to do according to all that is written in it. For then you will make your way prosperous, and then you will have good success. Have I not commanded you? Be strong and of good courage; do not be afraid, nor be dismayed, for the LORD your God is with you wherever you go. (Joshua 1:5–9)

God gave Joshua the greatest assurance He could: "I will not leave you nor forsake you." God could have promised Joshua continuous victory. He could have guaranteed him protection or wisdom. He could have even provided Joshua with state-of-the-art weapons for his soldiers. But when God pledged to Joshua His presence, He was offering him everything Joshua needed to be successful at every undertaking. God was not giving a gift; He was giving *Himself*.

Such an assurance left Joshua no cause for fear. Moreover, God said He would make His presence with Joshua obvious. Even Joshua's enemies would see it (Josh. 2:9–11; 8:9–10, 24)! "And the LORD said to Joshua, 'This day I will begin to exalt you in the sight of all Israel, that they may know that, as I was with Moses, so I will be with you'" (Josh. 3:7).

God was not giving a gift; He was giving *Himself*.

CONCEPT REFLECTION

CONCEPT: **God was not giving Joshua a gift; He was giving *Himself*.**

What is the value of receiving God's presence, as opposed to God's gifts, rewards, or tangible benefits?

_____

_____

_____

God immediately honored His promise. When the Israelites met their first major challenge under Joshua's leadership—crossing the Jordan River—God performed a spectacular miracle and brought them across on dry land (Josh. 3:15–17). Just as God had enabled Moses to master the barrier of the Red Sea, now God helped Joshua overcome the obstacle of the Jordan River.

When the people saw God's presence in Joshua's life just as they had witnessed it in Moses' life, they readily accepted Joshua's leadership. We read: "On that day the LORD exalted Joshua in the sight of all Israel; and they feared him, as they had feared Moses, all the days of his life" (Josh. 4:14). There is a profound life lesson here: God took care of Joshua's reputation. God exalted Joshua; Joshua didn't have to promote himself.

PERSONAL RESPONSE

How can you tell when it is *God* who is establishing a person's reputation, rather than the person himself?

_____

_____

_____

What does it look like when God exalts a person? In Joshua's case, people grew to highly regard him. This was not a grudging respect Joshua insisted upon because of his position. If Joshua had reduced himself to demanding respect from the people, he wouldn't have deserved it in the first place. God developed in the hearts and minds of the Israelites a deep, abiding esteem for His servant Joshua.

God exalts people in various ways. He honored the prophet Samuel by ensuring every prophecy he uttered came to pass (1 Sam. 3:19–20). He upheld Elijah by sending down fire when the beleaguered prophet called upon Him in front of the king and a host of hostile religious leaders (1 Kings 18:38). God protected Elisha's reputation when he was cruelly mocked by unruly youths (2 Kings 2:23–25). God blessed Job by giving him enormous wealth. God honored Moses in several ways, performing numerous spectacular miracles on his behalf.

Perhaps the greatest attestation to God's close relationship with Moses was the way Moses' face shone every time he had been in God's presence (Ex. 34:29–30). Seeing Moses' face glow was evidence to everyone that he enjoyed God's favor! Joshua's face did not glow as Moses' did, but he, too, communed intimately with God.

It is noteworthy that God exalted His servants in unique ways, according to their individual assignments. Moses had primarily been God's messenger to Pharaoh and to the Israelites. Joshua was a military commander. God affirmed Moses' role as His messenger by causing his face to shine after God instructed him. Likewise, God certified Joshua as a military commander by giving him victory in every battle. (The only exception was when Achan's sin brought God's judgment. [Josh. 7:10–26].)

> **If Joshua had reduced himself to demanding respect from the people, he wouldn't have deserved it in the first place.**

Just as the prophet Samuel's words always came to pass (1 Sam. 3:19), so Joshua emerged the victor in every conflict. People willingly deferred to Joshua's leadership because God's presence was evident by the outcome of every battle.

PERSONAL RESPONSE

What do you believe a leader should do when other people applaud his or her skills and abilities, or seek to exalt the leader to high levels of fame or status?

_____

_____

_____

_____

To what extent could the personal fame or status of a leader bring benefit to an organization?

_____

_____

_____

To what extent might the personal fame or status of a leader limit the good work of an organization?

_____

_____

_____

_____

We have known men and women from all walks of life who reflected God's special presence and blessing. No doubt you have too. Businesspeople, medical professionals, lawyers, and police officers have all testified to God's unique direction in their careers. Professional athletes have publicly attested to God's goodness. Parents have credited God for the blessing of children who wholeheartedly serve Christ as their Lord. Christian politicians have understood that God positioned them in a strategic place to make a godly impact on their nation.

God is looking for people today, just as He was in Joshua's day, who will trust Him, follow Him, and give Him the glory for all He does in their lives. God's presence in a life is powerful and unmistakable!

ADDED INSIGHT INTO SPIRITUAL LEADERSHIP

GOD-AUTHENTICATED LEADERS

God authenticates His chosen leaders in at least five ways:

1. God fulfills His promises to the leader and the leader's organization—leaders who continually present new ideas and visions for the future but who never see those dreams come to fruition are clearly presenting their own visions and not God's.

2. God vindicates the person's reputation over time, even though the leader may suffer criticism during the course of their work.

3. God changes the lives of those who follow—there's a clear sign of spiritual growth in the lives of those who follow a genuine spiritual leader.

4. God reveals Himself as the driving force behind the leader's agenda.

5. God produces the character of Christ in the leader—a person who is truly a spiritual leader is a person who is growing more and more like Christ.

Cite a specific way in which you believe God is authenticating you as a spiritual leader:

_____

_____

_____

_____

DAY THREE

JOSHUA POSSESSED THE SPIRIT OF WISDOM

What difference can God's Spirit make in a life? Joshua received the Spirit of wisdom and he was undefeatable (Num. 27:18). The Spirit took him beyond mere knowledge, giving him specific guidance to make the wisest decisions. God took the guesswork out of leadership for Joshua.

Joshua's willingness to trust God's wisdom, rather than his own knowledge, opened the floodgates of God's heavenly resources. Being able to recognize God's

God took the guesswork out of leadership for Joshua.

voice allowed Joshua to hear all God had to tell him. This gave Joshua a decisive advantage, both on the battlefield and off. That's the difference God's Spirit makes.

The great seduction for many Christian leaders is to exalt their own intelligence and their ability for rational thought to a level God never intends. Often, doing the reasonable thing is little more than an excuse to do what we think best without seeking the mind of the Lord on the subject. Woe to the organization that is guided merely by the best thinking of its leader!

Woe to the organization that is guided merely by the best thinking of its leader!

PERSONAL RESPONSE

How do you discern the difference between God's wisdom and your own rationality, common sense, or factual knowledge?

_____

_____

_____

_____

How might God's wisdom mesh with human rationality, common sense, and factual knowledge?

_____

_____

_____

How do you discern the difference between God's wisdom and your own conscience or voice of experience?

_____

_____

_____

_____

How might God's wisdom be manifested in a person's conscience?

_____

_____

_____

UNIT 4—GOD'S PRESENCE: THE SECRET TO SUCCESS

ADDED INSIGHT INTO
SPIRITUAL LEADERSHIP

MAN'S BEST THINKING ISN'T AS GOOD AS GOD'S PLAN

Spiritual leaders who develop their own visions, no matter how extensive, rather than understanding God's will, are settling for their best thinking instead of God's plans. It's a sure way to shortchange their followers. An example of this is found in Luke 9:51–56:

> Now it came to pass, when the time had come for Him to be received up, that He steadfastly set His face to go to Jerusalem, and sent messengers before His face. And as they went, they entered a village of the Samaritans, to prepare for Him. But they did not receive Him, because His face was set for the journey to Jerusalem. And when His disciples James and John saw this, they said, "Lord, do You want us to command fire to come down from heaven and consume them, just as Elijah did?" But He turned and rebuked them, and said, "You do not know what manner of spirit you are of. For the Son of Man did not come to destroy men's lives but to save them." And they went to another village.

What *were* James and John thinking! The Bible doesn't tell us the motives behind this statement by the overzealous "Sons of Thunder"—their comments may have been rooted in racism or pride or a false sense of needing to defend Jesus. They may have believed that with such a demonstration of power, other nearby villages would come to believe in Jesus. Whatever their reasoning was, Jesus rebuked the brothers. Their best thinking was completely out of line with the Father's plan.

Can you recall an incident in which man's best thinking fell far short of God's plan? _____

What were the results?

_____

_____

_____

Isaiah foretold that one day the Messiah would have God's Spirit upon Him:

> The Spirit of the LORD shall rest upon Him, the Spirit of wisdom and understanding, the Spirit of counsel and might, the Spirit of knowledge and of the

fear of the LORD. His delight is in the fear of the LORD,. and He shall not judge by the sight of His eyes, nor decide by the hearing of His ears; but with righteousness He shall judge the poor, and decide with equity for the meek of the earth; He shall strike the earth with the rod of His mouth, and with the breath of His lips He shall slay the wicked. Righteousness shall be the belt of His loins, and faithfulness the belt of His waist. (Isaiah 11:2–5)

The Spirit of wisdom is a profound gift for those who desire it and seek it. Those upon whom the Spirit rests need not face situations with their own limited wisdom and understanding. They do not have to determine the reality of their situation based on what their eyes see or their ears hear. They are not restricted to their physical senses or their own best logic. They have the counsel and wisdom of God available to them. Joshua made good use of this wisdom, and the results speak for themselves.

JOSHUA MEDITATED ON GOD'S WORD

Meditation hardly seems like the work of an industrious general. Yet God commanded Joshua to do just that if he hoped to succeed:

> Only be strong and very courageous, that you may observe to do according to all the law which Moses My servant commanded you; do not turn from it to the right hand or to the left, that you may prosper wherever you go. This Book of the Law shall not depart from your mouth, but you shall meditate in it day and night, that you may observe to do according to all that is written in it. For then you will make your way prosperous, and then you will have good success. (Joshua 1:7–8)

But how could a busy general command an army and administer a nation and still have time to meditate on anything? The hectic days would hardly afford opportunities for prolonged thought, let alone deep meditation. But God's command to meditate only sounds strange to the one who has never meditated.

Meditation is focused concentration. It does not require a lonely mountaintop or a convoluted body position. It does not call for a trance or a mystical chant. Biblical meditation involves pondering God's Word until He makes its full implication clear. It is staying in God's presence until God has helped you understand what His Word is saying to you.

Some biblical truths are self-evident; others require the Holy Spirit's illumination. A surface skimming of God's Word will not suffice for a leader who bears

Meditation is focused concentration . . . biblical meditation involves pondering God's Word until He makes its full implication clear.

UNIT 4—GOD'S PRESENCE: THE SECRET TO SUCCESS

great responsibility. Too much is at stake. Only a careful, thoughtful period of meditation will ensure that leaders grasp all the ramifications of God's Word for those they lead.

CONCEPT REFLECTION

CONCEPT: **Meditation is focused concentration. Biblical meditation involves pondering God's Word until God makes its full implication clear.**

What is the relationship between biblical meditation and the acquisition of God's wisdom?

_____

_____

_____

_____

_____

_____

Paradoxically, busy leaders facing significant time pressures assume they have no time to meditate on God's Word. Time is precious. Yet the wisest thing a spiritual leader can do is to seek God's wisdom. Careful evaluation of God's Word is a must for the sake of everyone involved. It is the leader's responsibility to help their people understand God's promises and respond to His invitations.

Busy leaders are people of action—others depend on them for prompt and timely decision-making. Yet history's greatest leaders have been able to screen out all distractions and to give their undivided attention to the issue at hand.

Likewise, spiritual leaders recognize that an unevaluated decision can bring disastrous and long-lasting consequences. The most potent tool at a spiritual leader's disposal is relentless, focused concentration on God's Word.

No crisis is pressing enough to prevent a leader from seeking God's perspective. A harried schedule should never hold a leader captive. Everyone is busy. But wise leaders understand the importance of meditation. They are proactive in scheduling time to focus, uninterrupted, on important issues.

The Bible is a storehouse packed full of wisdom. Unpacking its treasures takes time. God's Word holds answers leaders desperately need. The Scriptures can shed light on any situation. Why would a leader be foolhardy enough to ignore such a treasury of wisdom?

PERSONAL RESPONSE

What are the foremost obstacles that keep you from effective biblical meditation?

_____

_____

_____

How could you overcome those obstacles?

_____

_____

_____

God told Joshua: "Be strong and of good courage; do not be afraid, nor be dismayed, for the LORD your God is with you wherever you go" (Josh. 1:9). Was this important for Joshua to know? Absolutely. He was about to attempt the impossible. Thousands of people depended on him. He needed God to give him more than a sentimental, devotional thought. He needed a word from God that he could stake his life on.

Joshua ruminated over God's promise of His presence, meditating upon its practical implications. The coming days would bring numerous opportunities for fear and dismay. He had to be certain of the guarantees God had given him. Jesus made a similar promise to believers. He said, "And lo, I am with you always" (Matt. 28:20).

We need to grasp the enormity of this truth. How does this play out at our workplaces? What does it mean when we are admitted to the hospital? Is it still true when everyone seems to have abandoned us? How does this work practically in day-to-day situations? How can I know God hasn't forsaken me when everything in my life is going wrong? The Bible holds promises with enormous implications if we would take time to consider their potential to revolutionize our lives. Joshua did, and that is why he was so successful.

PERSONAL RESPONSE

Recall an experience in your life, or the life of someone you know, in which it was critically important to _know_ that the Lord was present in the midst of it:

_____

_____

_____

JOSHUA WAITED ON THE LORD

Leaders usually abhor waiting. They are typically doers. Most leaders would rather engage in *any* activity as long as they don't have to remain still! Waiting on God is different though. It *is* an activity, with a profound outcome. When you assume you must ultimately solve the problem or resolve the issue yourself, you feel compelled to take action. Knowing that God is responsible for the outcome of a situation or problem can turn waiting on Him into a relief. The response you make is determined by your view of God.

Waiting on God is actually a divine summons. It calls on the leader to acknowledge who is really in control. Waiting on God does not prescribe inactivity. Rather, it is an act of faith and obedience. Seeking God's direction takes more stamina than merely jumping rashly into action. If you think it doesn't take much effort to wait on the Lord, try it sometime! In every situation there is both a right thing to do and a right time to do it. Waiting on the Lord helps leaders get them both right!

Waiting on God is actually a divine summons.

CONCEPT REFLECTION

CONCEPT: **Waiting on God is actually a divine summons.**

What does God summon us to in times of waiting?

_____

_____

_____

King Saul revealed his spiritual immaturity by impatiently taking matters into his own hands rather than waiting on God. His brashness was his undoing (1 Sam. 13:1–14). God told him not to fight the Philistines until the prophet Samuel arrived to offer a sacrifice. A week went by with no sign of Samuel. Saul's soldiers nervously watched the enemy ranks swelling.

This was a litmus test of Saul's faith. How seriously did he take a word from God? Did he understand that even though he was the king, he could do *nothing* apart from God's strength? As the days passed, Saul's ranks diminished as more and more fearful soldiers deserted camp.

Finally, Saul couldn't stand it anymore. He took action himself and offered the sacrifice to God in his own way, rather than in the manner God had prescribed. His decision made sense to him, but it was a fatal error. In refusing to wait on God, Saul forfeited his right to be king.

Waiting on God is certainly a character-building exercise! Busy people are inundated with the voices of friends, colleagues, and clients. It takes an intentional effort to tune out every voice except God's. But personal and spiritual growth is the reward for doing so.

PERSONAL RESPONSE

How do you tend to respond when you are faced with a decision that needs to be made and you do not know what God desires? What *practically* do you do?

_____

_____

_____

A word of clarification is in order here. *Procrastination* and *waiting on the Lord* are two very different things!

Sometimes the biggest obstacle for a spiritual leader is not the problem itself, but the temptation to solve it alone. Spiritual leaders depend on a word from God. Without one they may be good leaders, but they will not be spiritual leaders. Spiritual leaders take God's Word and lead their followers to obey it. When a spiritual leader waits on God, a divine directive will come. And when it does, what the leader does next is critical.

Joshua was wise enough to understand that God knew far more than he did. Moreover, Joshua knew God intended to intervene on his behalf. It was therefore crucial to act in accordance with God's agenda. Doing things God's way would literally save thousands of soldiers' lives.

PERSONAL RESPONSE

How do you put yourself in the best possible position to hear what the Lord desires to say to you?

_____

_____

_____

But how do you wait on the Lord if you don't know what He is saying? The most important factor in waiting on the Lord is hearing from Him in the first place. Joshua spent a significant amount of his time seeking God's will. He was

Sometimes the biggest obstacle for a spiritual leader is not the problem itself, but the temptation to solve it alone.

an early riser. In those quiet morning hours, God spoke to His servant (Josh. 3:1; 6:12; 7:16; 8:10).

God does not exist to serve us. He does not shadow us, requesting an audience at our convenience. Joshua regularly made himself available to God, and God communicated with him. Each day brought significant challenges to the Israelites; they needed a leader who had been in the Lord's presence and knew His will. They depended on Joshua to trust in God's timing to help them.

Obedience means saying yes immediately, but it does not always call for immediate action. God's timing is perfect. A good work performed too early or too late can be more damaging than no work at all. Abraham rushed the birth of an heir, and it has cost his descendants ever since (Gen. 16:1–16).

The disciple Peter impetuously took a misguided stand for Jesus in the Garden of Gethsemane, and all he received for his devotion was a slave's ear and a rebuke from his Master (John 18:10–11). Joshua had to wait forty years before going into the promised land but when he finally entered in God's timing, his forces were invincible. The reward for waiting on God far exceeds the investment of patience required to do so.

Obedience means saying yes immediately, but it does not always call for immediate action.

PERSONAL RESPONSE

How do you determine God's *perfect timing* once you know He has called you to undertake a certain task or project?

_____

_____

_____

Identify and describe an experience in your life, or in the life of someone you know, in which *obedience* to God's precise timing led to the success of a project or relationship:

_____

_____

_____

Identify and describe an experience in your life, or in the life of someone you know, in which *disobedience* or a failure to discern God's precise timing led to the demise or diminished effectiveness of a project or relationship:

_____

_____

_____

Joshua Prayed

Modern leaders are known for a variety of things, but prayer is generally not one of them. Like waiting on God, prayer is often mistaken for inactivity. You have probably heard the phrase: "If you can't do anything else (give money, go to the mission field, and so forth), you can always pray!"

Prayer should never be viewed as a substitute for something of consequence. It is the most practical and effective thing people do. Yet busy leaders with hectic lives often consider prayer a luxury. Therefore it is often the first thing jettisoned once their calendars reach a saturation point. There are many administrators, but pitifully few intercessors.

Personal Response

What role does prayer play when you are seeking God's *wisdom*?

_____

_____

_____

How does prayer relate to biblical meditation?

_____

_____

_____

Joshua was a man of habitual prayer. When Israel suffered a demoralizing defeat against the city of Ai, Joshua's first response was to humbly seek God's explanation (Josh. 7:6–9). Joshua carefully processed his failure through prayer. God responded by revealing the reason for their loss and providing the means for victory (Josh. 7:10–15).

In the midst of a fierce battle against the Amorites, Joshua prayed for God to intervene in nature. Again, God responded, holding the sun in place and enabling the Israelites to gain a decisive victory (Josh. 10:12–14). Joshua was not a prophet or a priest. His primary ministry was not one of intercession. He was a general leading a dangerous and complicated invasion; but not even Moses, the great prophets Isaiah and Jeremiah, or powerful preachers like Peter and Paul ever saw the sun and moon affected in answer to their prayers!

Joshua's prayers were not spoken in generalities. He asked God to meet specific, tangible needs. And when God answered miraculously, Joshua received the answer not with surprise, but as a matter of course. The children of Israel

There are many administrators, but pitifully few intercessors.

Joshua carefully processed his failure through prayer.

UNIT 4—GOD'S PRESENCE: THE SECRET TO SUCCESS

must have gained a deep reverence for their leader who communed with God so confidently. They saw in Joshua the kind of meaningful, pragmatic prayer life that characterizes a true spiritual leader.

PERSONAL RESPONSE

Describe your prayer life, using several descriptive words or phrases:

_____

_____

_____

Is there anything you desire to change in your prayer life? If so, what?

_____

_____

_____

ADDED INSIGHT INTO SPIRITUAL LEADERSHIP

THE IMPORTANCE OF PRAYER

Prayer determines the effectiveness of a leader more than any other single thing a leader can do. If a leader will spend adequate time communing with God early in the morning, the people that leader encounters throughout the day will notice the difference.

The responsibility a leader has to *God* for the people who follow that leader is enormous. When leaders fully recognize that they are responsible to *God* for the people in their organization, they should feel compelled to pray—they should recognize that they cannot influence people, perceive accurately or accomplish God's goals, resolve difficult human-relations problems, deal with the stress of the leadership role, execute their role with wisdom, or have the right perspective on how to communicate with people apart from God's help!

Evaluate your own prayers for the people who follow you:

_____

_____

_____

DAY FIVE

JOSHUA HEARD GOD'S VOICE

It's quite obvious that God spoke to Joshua—often (Josh. 1:1; 3:7; 4:15; 5:15; 7:10; 8:1–2; 11:6; 13:1; 20:1). Joshua received a steady flow of specific instructions from God. This called on Joshua and his people for obedient responses. As they consistently obeyed God, they regularly experienced victory. Throughout the book of Joshua we find the following pattern: God spoke—Joshua obeyed—Joshua experienced success.

Many people, including some Bible scholars, claim that although God spoke to people like Joshua during biblical times, He does not speak to people today. Some say the Bible contains all the instructions people need. God's commands, along with the biblical principles found in Scripture, negate the need for a direct word from God.

However, many times you will face a situation where there is no specific command to apply to your circumstances. No biblical principle specifically tells you whether you should lay off employees when the economy hits a downturn. Neither is there a particular commandment to guide you to know whether you should take a certain business trip or fill a vacant volunteer position.

PERSONAL RESPONSE

How do you hear God's voice, or receive directives from the Lord?

_____

_____

_____

What role does prayer have in hearing God's voice?

_____

_____

_____

Those who follow God's law and look to biblical principles for their guidance are certain to find direction. But they will still miss out on the *relationship* they could have enjoyed as God applied His Word directly to their lives. For example, say you are invited to take a new job in a different city. Your teenage son is going through a tortuous time of spiritual questioning and rebellion. Would a new school and church bring a fresh start, or additional stress? Moving might bring your family to a dynamic new church and youth group; then again, it might not.

You seek biblical principles to help guide your decision. You have a spouse and other children so your decision is complex. There are relevant biblical principles regarding both parenting and stewardship. You are confused. Which principle applies here? Does one principle take precedence over another? More than anything, you want a clear word from God. There is a lot at stake here! Your family cannot afford for you to make a mistake.

Joshua frequently faced this type of situation. Because he was a leader, his decisions would have dramatic ramifications on others. He knew his thinking was not on the same level as God's (Isa. 55:8–9). So Joshua regularly spoke with God, and that's where he gained his perspective.

Scripture reveals that long before Joshua's time, God spoke to people. The book of Genesis tells of God speaking to people and many centuries after Joshua's time, the book of Revelation records God still communing with people. He spoke in numerous ways, but clearly He communicated with people. And He *still* does. The testimony of the saints through the centuries up to and including today is that God still pursues a personal relationship with His children, and He desires to give them His guidance.

Joshua regularly spoke with God, and that's where he gained his perspective.

CONCEPT REFLECTION

CONCEPT: Joshua regularly spoke with God, and that's where he gained his perspective.

How has your perspective of events in your life changed?

_____

_____

_____

How does God use prayer to build your relationship with Him?

_____

_____

_____

How has the Lord used prayer to change your perspective?

_____

_____

_____

Exactly *how* God spoke to Joshua is a biblical mystery. Did He use an audible voice or did He prompt Joshua's mind and heart? Scripture simply says, "The LORD spoke to Joshua" (Josh. 1:1). Obviously *how* God spoke was not considered important. *That* God spoke was crucial. God found a way to communicate His will to Joshua, Joshua understood what God said, and Joshua always responded in obedience.

Several times God gave Joshua military strategies he would not have known otherwise. God also revealed the identity of the culprit in Jericho who violated God's restrictions (Josh. 7:10–26). Hearing from God gave Joshua a decided advantage over his idol-worshiping opponents.

Hearing from God also removed any doubts Joshua might have had when going into battle. Once God appointed Joshua as a leader, Joshua had no need to fill out a spiritual gifts questionnaire to determine if he was equipped to lead. It didn't matter! God had just commissioned him as a leader and would guide him in each step he took.

Today there is an epidemic of evangelical idolatry. Idolatry is when people maintain substitutes for God. Rather than seeking Him, they pursue a principle. They don't respond immediately to God's voice. First, they take an inventory to see if they have the skills necessary to be obedient! People are trusting in doctrine rather than in God. People are placing their faith in their own leadership skills or training rather than in God's guidance. That's idolatry.

Today there is an epidemic of evangelical idolatry.

CONCEPT REFLECTION

CONCEPT: **Today there is an epidemic of evangelical idolatry.**

What can you do to avoid becoming guilty of evangelical idolatry?

_____

_____

_____

_____

Many Christians struggle to obey God, not because they are defiant, but because they are unsure how to hear from Him. If they clearly heard His voice, they would do what He said. But when you are uncertain how to recognize God's voice, you can become hesitant, afraid of making a mistake. Joshua was so familiar with God's voice that one word from God was enough to move him confidently forward. Hearing God's voice was the crux of Joshua's success as a spiritual leader.

UNIT 4—GOD'S PRESENCE: THE SECRET TO SUCCESS

Another Leader in God's Word

Daniel: Trusting God for Guidance

Daniel was faced with a tremendous difficulty. The king had asked his magicians, astrologers, sorcerers, and wisest advisers not only to tell him what he had dreamed, but to interpret the dream. When they responded that his request was impossible, the king said, "If you do not make known the dream to me, and its interpretation, you shall be cut in pieces, and your houses shall be made an ash heap" (Dan. 2:5). The magicians, astrologers, sorcerers, and wisest advisers could not fulfill what the king requested, of course, and in his fury, the king sent out a decree that they all be killed. The decree included Daniel and his companions.

When Daniel heard of the decree, he asked the king to give him time that he might tell the king the dream and its interpretation. The king agreed, and the Bible tells us: "Then Daniel went to his house, and made the decision known to Hananiah, Mishael, and Azariah, his companions, that they might seek mercies from the God of heaven concerning this secret, so that Daniel and his companions might not perish with the rest of the wise men of Babylon" (Dan. 2:17–18). In other words, the four of them agreed to pray in earnest! And that night, God revealed to Daniel the dream and the interpretation in a vision.

What is the most difficult situation you and your organization are facing today? _____ With whom might you agree in prayer that God will reveal His answer or solution? _____

Joshua Studied God's Ways

Joshua's appointment as Israel's new leader came with a profound promise. God assured him: "As I was with Moses, so I will be with you" (Josh. 1:5). Wrapped up in this magnificent promise was a history of miracles and victories along with more than one instance of discipline. Joshua had witnessed all this in Moses' period of leadership. In light of this word from God, it certainly behooved Joshua to review how God had specifically related to Moses!

When God first spoke to Moses, He identified Himself in terms of how He had walked with Moses' predecessors. He said, "I am the God of your father—the God of Abraham, the God of Isaac, and the God of Jacob" (Ex. 3:6). God was declaring that He was the same God the earlier patriarchs had followed. He would walk with Moses as He had related to the patriarchs. God never changes (Mal. 3:6).

The specific method God used to speak to Moses might vary greatly from the ways He spoke to the patriarchs. Abraham, Isaac, and Jacob never encountered a burning bush! But if Moses carefully studied the way God dealt with his forefathers, he would see that God would guide and sustain him too.

Now it was Joshua's turn. There was God's assurance He would make His presence obvious to Joshua. Joshua had witnessed the varied and unique ways He had manifested His presence to Moses. Now he would see God work mightily in his own life.

PERSONAL RESPONSE

Do you have a personal hero or heroine of the faith? _____

What have you learned from this leader? Identify several lessons:

_____

_____

_____

> **Spiritual leaders are wise to carefully study the ways God has worked through people's lives in Scripture and in history.**

Spiritual leaders are wise to carefully study the ways God has worked through people's lives in Scripture and in history so they know how God might use their lives for His kingdom as well.

We have plenty of reason to study the Scriptures. Through the millennia God has worked powerfully through the lives of ordinary people. God's activity in the lives of His people is evident not only in biblical history, but throughout two thousand years of Christian history as well. We should confidently assume that just as God was with Moses and David and Peter and Paul, so He will be with us.

ADDED INSIGHT INTO SPIRITUAL LEADERSHIP

GETTING GOD'S IDEAS

Man's best ideas can never approach God's perfect plans. Read what God's Word says about this:

- Isaiah 55:8–9: "For My thoughts are not your thoughts, nor are your ways My ways," says the LORD. "For as the heavens are higher than the earth, so are My ways higher than your ways, and My thoughts than your thoughts."

- Proverbs 3:5–6: "Trust in the LORD with all your heart, and lean not on your own understanding; in all your ways acknowledge Him, and He shall direct your paths."

- Jeremiah 33:2–3: "Thus says the LORD who made it, the LORD who formed it to establish it (the LORD is His name): 'Call to Me, and I will answer you, and show you great and mighty things, which you do not know.'"

What do you perceive God is saying to you personally through these passages in His Word?

_____

_____

_____

GOD'S PRESENCE MAKES ALL THE DIFFERENCE

Joshua had many skills and talents that helped him to function effectively as a leader. Yet those skills alone cannot explain his phenomenal success. Only God can. God's presence was unmistakably obvious, not only to God's people but even to unbelievers. And that presence made all the difference.

As Joshua yielded himself to God's guidance, God was pleased to use his life for His divine purposes. God often spoke to Joshua and made sure he knew His will. Joshua meditated upon the words God spoke. Joshua knew that his life, and the lives of his countrymen, depended upon his understanding and obeying God's word.

Joshua prayed regularly. He waited upon God. He observed how God walked with those who had gone before him. He sought to have a close walk with God himself. Joshua was not satisfied with anything less than God's manifest presence in his life. And God was active in Joshua's life. The Scriptures bear testimony to the astounding success God's presence made in the life of one servant who listened to Him and obeyed what he heard.

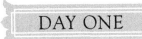

UNIT 5

OBEDIENCE THAT
GOES THE DISTANCE

> *For Joshua did not draw back his hand, with which he stretched out the spear, until he had utterly destroyed all the inhabitants of Ai. Only the livestock and the spoil of that city Israel took as booty for themselves, according to the word of the LORD which He had commanded Joshua. So Joshua burned Ai and made it a heap forever, a desolation to this day.*
>
> JOSHUA 8:26–28

Joshua was a respected general, the nation's top leader, yet he clearly understood his role as a servant of God. He never confused who the leader was in his relationship with his Lord. Joshua demonstrated a radical subservience to the commands of his King. Joshua yielded to God, obeyed God, accepted hard assignments, and Joshua's obedience was unflinching.

DAY ONE

JOSHUA YIELDED TO GOD

An unusual event in Joshua's life occurred on the eve of his famous attack on Jericho:

And it came to pass, when Joshua was by Jericho, that he lifted his eyes and looked, and behold, a Man stood opposite him with His sword drawn in His hand. And Joshua went to Him and said to Him, "Are You for us or for our adversaries?" So He said, "No, but as Commander of the army of the LORD I have now come." And Joshua fell on his face to the earth and worshiped, and said to Him, "What does my Lord say to His servant?" Then the Commander of the LORD's army said to Joshua, "Take your sandal off your foot, for the place where you stand is holy." And Joshua did so. (Joshua 5:13–15)

Jericho symbolized the very thing that had terrified ten Hebrew spies forty years earlier. It was a walled city protected by menacing soldiers. It looked invincible. Jericho was the ultimate test for the Israelites. They had finally entered the promised land, but they had yet to fight the enemy. The following day would bring the first major test to this generation of Israelite warriors.

The evening before the battle, Joshua carefully surveyed the fortified city. His gaze suddenly fell upon an impressive-looking soldier with sword in hand. A drawn sword indicated battle-readiness. Joshua boldly confronted the stranger to determine if he was friend or foe.

Joshua discovered the stranger was neither for Jericho nor for Israel—he was God's servant. Joshua's heavenly visitor was commander of the Lord's army. A military man, Joshua immediately recognized one who carried greater authority than he. Joshua stood before one who far outranked him and whose army was infinitely more powerful than his.

Their interchange is reminiscent of two similar biblical encounters. Jacob met a heavenly messenger one night as he waited at the ford of the river Jabbock to meet his estranged brother Esau. Unlike Joshua, Jacob wrestled with his divine visitor all evening (Gen. 32:22–32). For whatever reason, when confronted with God's messenger, Jacob's first impulse was to fight.

Likewise, when Moses encountered God in a burning bush, his natural instinct was to resist. Moses argued against God's will until he provoked the Lord's anger (Ex. 4:14). Jacob was a deceiver—a conniver who sought the advantage over others. Moses lacked confidence. He was aware of his many inadequacies, and he was convinced God was making a mistake by calling him into His service.

Joshua's military experience taught him to recognize authority. He knew subordinates did not argue with their superiors. The moment he recognized whose presence he was in, there was no wrestling or arguing. There was only obedience.

PERSONAL RESPONSE

What tends to be your response to those who have more authority than you do? For example: Do you resist their commands and fight or compete with them, or obey their commands and respect their authority? _____

What consequences—in the long run—does your response generally trigger?

_____

_____

_____

Resisting God is a costly venture. For the remainder of his life, Jacob's limping gait was a visible reminder of his stubbornness (Gen. 32:31). Moses had to speak for God through Aaron throughout the rest of his ministry (Ex. 4:14–16). On the other hand, God chose to mightily bless Joshua's leadership throughout his life.

Life affords numerous opportunities for believers to prove their allegiance to God. The same God who encountered Jacob, Moses, Joshua, and dozens of other Bible characters, confronts each Christian with His will.

Resistance always comes at a price. Scores of troubled people have shared with us that God called them into ministry, but they resisted and put off their ministerial training for numerous practical reasons. They spent their lives on the sidelines when they knew they should be serving God in full-time ministry.

God prompted others to restore broken relationships, but their pride prevented reconciliation until it was too late. Fortunately, God is gracious, and He will restore us if we will obey what we know He is asking us to do today. But many lost opportunities are irretrievable.

CONCEPT REFLECTION

CONCEPT: Resisting God is a costly venture.

Cite an example in your life, or in the life of someone you know, in which this was manifested:

_____

_____

_____

The New Testament tells of a man in Jesus' day who, much like Joshua, displayed remarkable faith (Matt. 8:5–13). A Gentile centurion approached Jesus on behalf of his ailing servant. Jesus offered to accompany the noble soldier to heal his servant, but the man humbly demurred:

> Lord, I am not worthy that You should come under my roof. But only speak a
> word, and my servant will be healed. For I also am a man under authority, hav-
> ing soldiers under me. And I say to this one, "Go," and he goes; and to
> another, "Come," and he comes; and to my servant, "Do this," and he does it.
> (Matthew 8:8–9)

This man recognized authority! For such men there is no begrudging or questioning a superior's commands. There is only submission. Jesus was amazed at the veteran soldier's faith and richly rewarded his servitude (Matt. 8:10, 13).

People sometimes speak of "wrestling" with God: "I know God wants me to lead a Bible study in my home, but I have been wrestling with Him about it because I don't feel adequate for the task." Or, "I sense God wants me to accept a job transfer, but I have been wrestling with Him because it means moving away from my friends and relatives."

Wrestling is not a legitimate step in the process of seeking God's will. It is blatant disobedience. Those who speak of wrestling with God do not know Him. God is not an equal to be resisted. He is God, and we must yield to Him.

> **God is not an equal to be resisted. He is God, and we must yield to Him.**

PERSONAL RESPONSE

What are some of the factors that keep a person from instant obedience?

_____

_____

_____

_____

_____

_____

Do any of these factors count in God's eyes? _____

To respond appropriately to God's will, we must understand His nature. *God is love* (1 John 4:8). He cannot and will not act out of any motive but perfect love. Everything God will ever say to you is an expression of His love. Even when He disciplines you and convicts you of your sin, it is because He loves you (Heb. 12:6–7). Why would anyone resist an expression of perfect love? It is ludicrous, to say nothing of costly, to argue with Him.

God is omniscient. He is all-knowing. He sees the future. He understands our past and our present in minute detail. His wisdom is infinite. To what purpose would anyone argue with a God such as this?

Finally, *God is omnipotent.* He is all-powerful. Consider the words of the apostle John as he described his vision of the risen Christ upon His throne:

> Immediately I was in the Spirit; and behold, a throne set in heaven, and One sat on the throne. And He who sat there was like a jasper and a sardius stone in appearance; and there was a rainbow around the throne, in appearance like an emerald. Around the throne were twenty-four thrones, and on the thrones I saw twenty-four elders sitting, clothed in white robes; and they had crowns of gold on their heads. And from the throne proceeded lightnings, thunder-

ings, and voices. Seven lamps of fire were burning before the throne, which are the seven Spirits of God. Before the throne there was a sea of glass, like crystal. And in the midst of the throne, and around the throne, were four living creatures full of eyes in front and in back. The first living creature was like a lion, the second living creature like a calf, the third living creature had a face like a man, and the fourth living creature was like a flying eagle. The four living creatures, each having six wings, were full of eyes around and within. And they do not rest day or night, saying:

"Holy, holy, holy, Lord God Almighty, who was and is and is to come!"

Whenever the living creatures give glory and honor and thanks to Him who sits on the throne, who lives forever and ever, the twenty-four elders fall down before Him who sits on the throne and worship Him who lives forever and ever, and cast their crowns before the throne, saying:

"You are worthy, O Lord, to receive glory and honor and power; for You created all things, and by Your will they exist and were created." (Revelation 4:2–11)

Is there any mention of resistance or struggle? Of course not. That would be absurd! The Lord of heaven and earth is exalted upon His throne. No one complains that they are not gifted to sing "Holy, Holy, Holy"! No one begrudges the length of the worship service. No one insists they cannot afford to cast their crowns at His feet. In heaven, the saints will humbly worship and obey their Lord, not because they have to, but because when they see God as He truly is, no other response will cross their minds!

PERSONAL RESPONSE

To what extent might a failure to obey *quickly* be an indicator that a person has a faulty understanding of God's love, omniscience, or omnipotence?

_____

_____

_____

We mortals have yet to gaze upon our risen Lord. The evidence of His existence and greatness is everywhere around us, but it still requires faith to believe Him and to obey Him. Some feel they can argue with God because they have yet to learn what He is truly like. However, those who really come to know Christ will deny themselves, take up their crosses, and follow Him (Matt. 10:37–39; 16:24–25; Luke 14:26–27). No other response befits a follower of Christ (Isa. 6:1–5).

DAY TWO

JOSHUA OBEYED GOD

Joshua was not a halfhearted believer. His thoroughness is evident in an event that occurred after the Israelites crossed the Jordan River into Canaan. God told Joshua to circumcise all the Israelite males (Josh. 5:2). The Hebrew children born during the forty years of wandering in the wilderness had not been circumcised as their fathers had.

Before God would use them to establish a nation in Canaan, He wanted all the men to physically bear the sign of His covenant with them. From a pragmatic perspective, this does not appear to be the best timing for such an exercise in obedience. Circumcising all the adult males after having just entered enemy territory would have left the army vulnerable to attack.

Joshua might have been excused for waiting for a safer and more convenient time to take care of this issue. But his primary concern was not safety or convenience; it was obedience. Joshua wisely concluded the best place for his army was in the center of God's will.

His primary concern was not safety or convenience; it was obedience.

BIBLE CONTEMPLATION

> ### MATTHEW 16:24–25
> *"Then Jesus said to His disciples, 'If anyone desires to come after Me, let him deny himself, and take up his cross, and follow Me. For whoever desires to save his life will lose it, but whoever loses his life for My sake will find it.'"*

What does it mean to deny oneself and take up a cross and follow Christ?

_____

_____

_____

Since God first established His covenant with Abraham (Gen. 17:10–14), circumcision signified that a Hebrew male belonged to God's people. Other nations also practiced circumcision, but usually on adults and for other reasons. Abraham's descendants were all to be circumcised as infants and to grow up with the physical reminder that they belonged to God.

PERSONAL RESPONSE

Is there an area of your life in which you know you are *not* fully obeying the Lord? What do you need to do to come into full obedience?

_____

_____

_____

_____

_____

_____

Moses was meticulous in most areas of his walk with God, but he seems to have lapsed in the area of circumcision. After meeting with God at the burning bush, Moses traveled toward Egypt. On the way, God almost took his life because he had failed to circumcise his son:

> And it came to pass on the way, at the encampment, that the LORD met him and sought to kill him. Then Zipporah took a sharp stone and cut off the foreskin of her son and cast it at Moses' feet, and said, "Surely you are a husband of blood to me!" So He let him go. Then she said, "You are a husband of blood!"—because of the circumcision. (Exodus 4:24–26)

Moses' wife, Zipporah, was a Midianite. Midianites circumcised adult males just before their wedding. Perhaps Moses was putting off his son's circumcision until his wedding day to satisfy his wife. Whatever the reason, God expected the leader of His people to adhere to His commands. Failing to do so almost cost Moses his life.

It's not clear whether God explicitly commanded circumcision of Hebrew children during the forty years they lived in the desert, but none of the Israelites were circumcised during Moses' term of leadership. In light of Moses' failure to have his son or any of the other males circumcised, Joshua's immediate obedience to God's instruction is even more impressive. He understood that circumcision represented the people's commitment to God's covenant.

Before they invaded the promised land, every man was to signify his total commitment to God. In calling for every male's circumcision, Joshua surely encountered some resistance. He also risked his popularity as a leader. But when it came to following God's commands, Joshua was single-minded.

ADDED INSIGHT INTO
SPIRITUAL LEADERSHIP

TWO DIFFERENT PERSPECTIVES

Some leaders make their own plans and agendas and ask God to bless them. The godly leader seeks to know and implement God's plans and agendas.

Which approach does God honor? Which approach brings glory to God? God honors and blesses the person who seeks to know His will and do it. In like manner, God honors the leader who seeks to know His will for a group of people and leads them to implement it to the best of their ability.

Identify a particular difficulty or problem situation you are currently facing. Do you need to change the way you are approaching your own problem-solving and decision-making processes? If so, what changes do you perceive you need to make?

_____

_____

_____

_____

_____

_____

_____

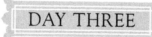

DAY THREE

JOSHUA ACCEPTED
HARD ASSIGNMENTS

Two important truths Joshua lived by are two of the most difficult realities for modern Christians to understand and accept: (1) God will eventually judge everyone who sins against Him; (2) God commands His people to remain separate from spiritual rebels, lest they be drawn into the same destructive lifestyle that inevitably brings about God's judgment. Only by clearly understanding the importance of both these truths can we appreciate what God told Joshua to do to the inhabitants of Canaan.

Joshua's job, as happens in all leadership positions, put him into some tough situations. The times in which he lived were barbaric, and life was often extremely difficult. As the Israelites approached Jericho, God commanded them to refrain from taking any plunder after their victory. Everything in Jericho—their first conquest in Canaan—was to be dedicated to God as a holy sacrifice (Josh. 6:18–19). Every living thing within Jericho was to be destroyed, except for Rahab and her relatives (Josh. 6:22–23).

God's command appears unduly harsh to us and seemingly far removed from the love Jesus showed the notorious sinner Zacchaeus and the gentle forgiveness the Savior offered the adulterous woman (Luke 19:1–10; John 8:1–11). Why would the same loving God instruct His people to withhold mercy from their Canaanite foes?

It seems to fly in the face of Jesus' command to love our enemies (Matt. 5:38–45). Yet there is a vast difference between the manner in which Jesus commanded His disciples to respond to personal injuries and the way God dealt with nations that repeatedly defied His holy standards.

Canaan was infested with idolatry and the grossest forms of immorality. The people embraced idol worship to hideous extremes. Farmers desiring rain for their crops and a lucrative harvest would sacrifice their own children on an altar in an effort to win their idol's favor. Their depraved worship included prostitution and immoral acts as a part of religious services.

The pagan religion encouraged every carnal and debased practice God had condemned. Canaanite worship was the vulgar antithesis of what holy God prescribed for His people. Unless the people of Canaan repented, God would ultimately judge them.

God made a prophetic statement to Abraham centuries earlier that would eventually come to pass in Joshua's day. God was fully aware of the moral and spiritual depravity of the Amorites who inhabited the promised land. God told Abraham his descendants would suffer a difficult sojourn in a distant country for four hundred years, "for the iniquity of the Amorites is not yet complete" (Gen. 15:16).

God was being merciful to the inhabitants of Canaan. Their blatant sensuality was an abomination to His holiness. Yet God declared that their sins had not yet reached full maturity, the point at which God's righteousness would demand punishment. In fact, God granted them four hundred additional years to turn from the wickedness of their ways.

Only an infinitely gracious and loving God who does not desire that anyone perish would be so lenient (2 Peter 3:9). In our day, it is sobering to realize Christ has delayed His final return and judgment for two thousand years so that every person has the opportunity to respond to His love and to be saved from the consequences of his or her sin.

> ### 2 PETER 3:9–10
>
> *"The Lord is not slack concerning His promise, as some count slackness, but is longsuffering toward us, not willing that any should perish but that all should come to repentance. But the day of the Lord will come as a thief in the night, in which the heavens will pass away with a great noise, and the elements will melt with fervent heat; both the earth and the works that are in it will be burned up."*

How do you balance the long-suffering nature of a loving God and the absolute judgment of a righteous God?

_____

_____

_____

What are the implications for your own life?

_____

_____

_____

By the time Joshua arrived in Canaan with the Israelites, the Canaanites' opportunity to repent was finally exhausted. Joshua and his soldiers were to be the instruments of God's judgment on a people who mocked and rejected Him, even after centuries of receiving His mercy.

God did not always command the Israelites to exterminate everyone they fought. This was not the routine way Israelite armies treated their enemies once they inhabited Canaan. Often people would be given the opportunity to surrender and, if they did not, women and children would still generally be spared.

Yet God intended for Jericho, the first city, to be utterly destroyed. Not only was God determined to judge the sinful inhabitants and to strike paralyzing fear in the hearts of their allies, He was also deeply concerned that Israel not be morally or spiritually contaminated by the influence of the idol-worshiping Canaanites.

God repeatedly urged His people not to intermarry with those who practiced pagan religions. Marrying outside their faith would have a spiritually deadening effect upon His people. God commanded them:

Do not defile yourselves with any of these things; for by all these the nations are defiled, which I am casting out before you. For the land is defiled; therefore I visit the punishment of its iniquity upon it, and the land vomits out its inhabitants. You shall therefore keep My statutes and My judgments, and shall not commit any of these abominations, either any of your own nation or any stranger who dwells among you (for all these abominations the men of the land have done, who were before you, and thus the land is defiled), lest the land vomit you out also when you defile it, as it vomited out the nations that were before you. For whoever commits any of these abominations, the persons who commit them shall be cut off from among their people. Therefore you shall keep My ordinance, so that you do not commit any of these abominable customs which were committed before you, and that you do not defile yourselves by them: I am the LORD your God. (Leviticus 18:24–30)

PERSONAL RESPONSE

What difficulties have you encountered in trying to remain morally and spiritually uncontaminated by the society or culture in which you live?

_____

_____

_____

What does it mean to you to remove yourself from spiritually deadening behaviors and associations?

_____

_____

_____

God's message both to His people and to the idolatrous Canaanites was clear and powerful. He was declaring total, implacable war on the sinful and idolatrous lifestyle of those who rejected Him. God left no room for discussion or compromise. If allowed to remain in Canaan, the idol-worshipers would be fierce enemies of the Israelites. They would have little interest in sharing Israel's religion. Instead they would provide enticing temptations for compromise and immorality.

Joshua eliminated the leading religious leaders of the idolatrous nations in Canaan. God was divesting the promised land of the idolatry that would tempt the Israelites toward their own destruction. It may seem incomprehensible that God used Joshua as an instrument to bring death to so many. But God's ways are not our ways (Isa. 55:8–9).

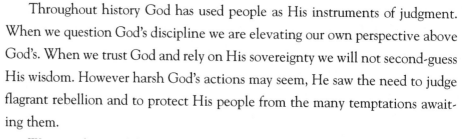

When we question God's discipline we are elevating our own perspective above God's.

Throughout history God has used people as His instruments of judgment. When we question God's discipline we are elevating our own perspective above God's. When we trust God and rely on His sovereignty we will not second-guess His wisdom. However harsh God's actions may seem, He saw the need to judge flagrant rebellion and to protect His people from the many temptations awaiting them.

We must be careful not to think we are more compassionate and gracious to sinners than God is! We must also be cautious in placing our concern on the side of the sinner rather than in the sovereignty of God. God is infinitely loving, but He is also absolutely just. There comes a time when God will no longer delay bringing judgment on those who deserve it (Jer. 15:1).

It is a natural instinct to become uneasy when God disciplines someone. At times a church must respond firmly to a wayward member who blatantly sins and refuses to repent. The inevitable reaction of some members is: "Yes, they sinned, but who hasn't? Who are we to judge? But for the grace of God we would do the same thing!"

Listen carefully: *compassion for a sinner is absolutely crucial, but misguided compassion can lead us to flagrantly oppose the work God is doing in our midst.* Excusing another's continuous rebellion actually harms them more than it helps them. Our concern ought to always be with God and His redemptive activity. We do not help fellow Christians by interfering when God is disciplining them.

CONCEPT REFLECTION

CONCEPT: Compassion for a sinner is absolutely crucial, but misguided compassion can lead us to flagrantly oppose the work God is doing in our midst.

Can you recall an experience or example in which you have witnessed this directly or indirectly?

_____

_____

_____

_____

The New Testament also warns of the dangers of allowing sinners to corrupt God's people: "Do not be unequally yoked together with unbelievers. For what fellowship has righteousness with lawlessness? And what communion has light with darkness? And what accord has Christ with Belial? Or what part has a believer with an unbeliever?" (2 Cor. 6:14). Long after Joshua's time, God still commands us as His people not to link our lives with unbelievers, lest they draw us away from our allegiance to God.

We have known parents who never taught their children the magnitude of this charge. When their child began dating an unbeliever, the parents did not urge them to break off their relationship and heed God's counsel. The well-meaning parents did not want to appear harsh or judgmental. After their child's marriage, the wisdom of God's warning became increasingly apparent.

Significant differences of opinion arose between the young couple regarding how to raise the children, whether to attend church, how to use their money, and what moral standards to establish for their home. The Christian spouse suffered the lonely experience of single-handedly carting the kids off to church week after week under the apathetic gaze of the unbelieving spouse. Eventually the fundamental differences in values and priorities led to a heart-breaking divorce.

The parents who thought God's injunction was too severe to impress on their child were forced to watch helplessly as their precious child and grand-children suffered the agony of marriage breakdown. While God's commands can sometimes seem demanding, they are always motivated by love and they are always for our good.

PERSONAL RESPONSE

What commands of God are the most difficult for you to obey? Why?

_____

_____

_____

What does your reluctance in obedience reveal about your beliefs about God's nature and His desires for you?

_____

_____

_____

Joshua was never squeamish about following God's most difficult commands. Joshua was not a malicious, vindictive man who enjoyed destroying cities. But he understood that when God placed people under judgment, their punishment was to be thorough:

> **While God's commands can sometimes seem demanding, they are always motivated by love and they are always for our good.**

But of the cities of these peoples which the LORD your God gives you as an inheritance, you shall let nothing that breathes remain alive, but you shall utterly destroy them: the Hittite and the Amorite and the Canaanite and the Perizzite and the Hivite and the Jebusite, just as the LORD your God has commanded you, lest they teach you to do according to all their abominations which they have done for their gods, and you sin against the LORD your God. (Deuteronomy 20:16–18)

After Jericho's destruction, God instructed Joshua to raze the nearby city of Ai. Joshua's forces were initially defeated because of sin in his ranks, but Joshua attacked the small city a second time. Joshua informed his warriors that as long as he held up his javelin, they were to fight the enemy to the death.

Joshua held up his javelin until there were no enemy survivors (Josh. 8:25–26). Over and over again, the book of Joshua tells us Joshua was called upon to leave no survivors (Josh. 6:24; 8:26; 10:20, 28; 11:14). To carry out such an onerous assignment, Joshua had to cling tightly to his unwavering faith in God's righteous wisdom.

ADDED INSIGHT INTO SPIRITUAL LEADERSHIP

GIFTS OF RESOURCES

Wise leaders do not allow the availability of resources to determine the direction of their organization. As a general rule, resources should follow vision, not determine it. Leaders must first determine God's vision for their organization and then marshal the necessary resources to achieve it. Foolish leaders will thoughtlessly accept resources and then try to piece together a vision that uses the resources they have accumulated.

Have you or someone you know ever received a gift of resources that came with strings attached—strings that may have been contrary to a God-given vision? _____ What were the results of accepting or not accepting such a gift of resources?

_____

_____

_____

_____

JOSHUA'S OBEDIENCE WAS UNFLINCHING

When the Israelites approached Jericho, God declared the city under the ban—every living creature was to be destroyed and no loot was to be kept. Everything was to be a holy sacrifice to God. A man named Achan spied a beautiful garment and some silver and gold, and he couldn't resist hiding them in his tent (Josh. 7:21). No one else knew of Achan's store of contraband.

It appeared the Israelites had been overwhelmingly successful. God miraculously brought the walls of Jericho crumbling down as He had promised. The Israelites quickly overcame the stunned resisters, and the city fell into their hands. Yet, in the midst of the victory celebrations, Achan was surreptitiously stashing his loot. Some of the most costly sins are committed in the shadow of God's greatest works. Perhaps it was people such as Achan to whom the apostle John referred when he said, "They went out from us, but they were not of us" (1 John 2:19).

We have all known of such situations—perhaps it was a congregation flourishing under God's blessing. Attendance was multiplying. People were coming to know Christ. Broken families were being restored. Mission projects were under way. Then came a stunning revelation—the pastor was involved in sexual immorality. Shock reverberated among the congregation and the community.

It seemed incomprehensible that someone in the center of God's redemptive activity could be tempted to sin so grievously. But it is possible, and tragically, it happens often. Leaders should never underestimate their own vulnerability to sin, even when they are at a point of great personal success. We always fall farthest from our highest point.

CONCEPT REFLECTION

CONCEPT: Leaders should never underestimate their own vulnerability to sin.

Is there a particular sin that you don't believe is a sin to you personally because of the favor or blessing you have experienced from God? In other words, is there an activity or attitude that you believe applies to others but not to you because you are God's chosen leader?

Some of the most costly sins are committed in the shadow of God's greatest works.

Leaders should never underestimate their own vulnerability to sin.

_____

_____

What are the ultimate consequences if you indulge in that sin?

_____

_____

_____

How difficult is it to identify one's own justification of sin?

_____

_____

_____

How important is it to remain in a position of accountability to others?

_____

_____

_____

Ananias and Sapphira were privileged to be members of the first church in Jerusalem. They had Peter, James, and John as their pastors and godly men such as Stephen as their deacons. Three thousand people were added to their church in just one day (Acts 2:41)! Needless to say, God was working mightily! Miracles were a frequent occurrence.

But in the midst of all of God's activity, this couple was consumed with pride. They allowed their greed to overtake them, and it led them to publicly dishonor the Holy Spirit. The result was death for them both (Acts 5:1–11). Committing blasphemy in the midst of God's greatest work is the insidious work of sin in a person's heart.

Ananias's and Sapphira's consequences were instantaneous. Not so with Achan. His sin remained hidden in his tent until the Israelites confronted their next opponent, the city of Ai. This minor city should have presented minimal challenge. Only a small contingent of Israelite soldiers was considered necessary to secure a victory. Yet, to their profound dismay, the Israelites were soundly defeated. This was Joshua's only recorded defeat, and he didn't take it well!

Then Joshua tore his clothes, and fell to the earth on his face before the ark of the LORD until evening, he and the elders of Israel; and they put dust on

UNIT 5—OBEDIENCE THAT GOES THE DISTANCE

their heads. And Joshua said, "Alas, Lord GOD, why have You brought this people over the Jordan at all—to deliver us into the hand of the Amorites, to destroy us? Oh, that we had been content, and dwelt on the other side of the Jordan! O Lord, what shall I say when Israel turns its back before its enemies? For the Canaanites and all the inhabitants of the land will hear it, and surround us, and cut off our name from the earth. Then what will You do for Your great name?" (Joshua 7:6–9)

Considering the Israelites only lost a few dozen men in the skirmish, Joshua's response appears almost melodramatic. But Joshua's confidence in God had been absolute. He fully believed that when God marched with him into battle, he was invincible. God had promised: "Every place that the sole of your foot will tread upon I have given you . . . no man shall be able to stand before you all the days of your life" (Josh. 1:3, 5).

The possibility of defeat never crossed Joshua's mind as long as he followed God's will. This setback deeply troubled him. He had obeyed God's instructions and was still defeated. What assurance was there for his future? Furthermore, when word spread across Canaan that it was indeed possible to defeat God's people, all their enemies would quickly attack them with a vengeance.

The second half of God's promise was that if the Israelites were not faithful, He would ensure their continual loss in battle (Deut. 28:7, 25). Though Joshua was unaware of Achan's treachery, he now knew the bitter taste of defeat. Joshua must have been bewildered and horrified at the thought of having God as his enemy. Joshua's entire view of God was momentarily shaken. Then Joshua heard from God and, as always, that put everything into perspective.

The possibility of defeat never crossed Joshua's mind as long as he followed God's will.

PERSONAL RESPONSE

What is the possibility that a defeat in your life is the direct consequence of sin—yours or another person's?

_____

_____

_____

How do you evaluate this possibility?

_____

_____

_____

God urged His despondent general: "Get up! Why do you lie thus on your face? Israel has sinned" (Josh. 7:10–11). Significantly, God did not say, "Achan has sinned." All of God's people were to face the consequences of one man's sin. God could have identified the culprit, and Joshua could have discreetly punished him. Yet God caused the entire nation to go through the extremely public process of discovering the traitorous sinner.

Tribe by tribe, clan by clan, family by family, the people of Israel watched as God disclosed the guilty person and pronounced judgment on him: "Then it shall be that he who is taken with the accursed thing shall be burned with fire, he and all that he has, because he has transgressed the covenant of the LORD, and because he has done a disgraceful thing in Israel" (Josh. 7:15).

Everyone knew what was at stake for the one condemned. As the entire nation watched, they witnessed the gravity of sin. No one could miss the way God thoroughly and stringently treated the disobedience of His people. God used this crisis as a profound deterrent for every Israelite household.

When God finally identified Achan as the culprit, Joshua was left with the incredibly difficult task of putting him and his family to death. Achan was from the tribe of Judah, of the Zarhites. He would have had many relatives and friends among the Israelites.

Surely the people were shaken by such a severe punishment. After all, the contraband had been discovered and the sin confessed. Yet God treated this disregard for His word with utmost severity. He made a dramatic example of Achan and left no room for doubt that His word was always to be treated with reverence and followed scrupulously.

Jericho had been the first enemy stronghold the Israelites had attacked in Canaan, and already one of God's people had flagrantly sinned. If the Israelites were going to successfully conquer the promised land, they would have to be convinced that only total obedience was acceptable to God. Absolute compliance to God's word was the key to their success. And so God punished Achan in such a dramatic way that every Israelite got the message.

CONCEPT REFLECTION

CONCEPT: Joshua obviously feared God far more than he feared men.

Describe a difficult challenge you are currently facing:

_____

_____

_____

What does it mean to fear God more than you fear people in this situation?

_____

_____

_____

Obeying God's decree put Joshua in a heart-wrenching situation. Killing enemy soldiers in hand-to-hand combat was one thing. Slaying one of your own people was quite another. Everyone looked to Joshua to see what he would do. Moses had dealt with his share of detractors and critics. Joshua could be sure that if he acted, many people might consider him heartless and cruel. Yet not to follow through would gain him God's displeasure.

Joshua obviously feared God far more than he feared people. We see no hesitation. No questioning God (Josh. 7:24–26). In fact, on that morning Joshua rose early to begin the difficult job (Josh. 7:16). It was a harsh, gruesome task, but Joshua and the people did it promptly and completely.

After Achan's death, there is no record of a similar breach of obedience among God's people throughout the remainder of Joshua's leadership. It is a frightening thing for God to use the example of your life as a deterrent for others.

We are not at liberty to pick and choose which of God's commands we will obey. Some words from God are welcome and agreeable. Others call for great effort and sacrifice. Joshua never seems to have distinguished between the two. Whether the command was easy to carry out or whether it was arduous, Joshua was equally zealous.

It is a frightening thing for God to use the example of your life as a deterrent for others.

DAY FIVE

JOSHUA SOMETIMES BLEW IT

Joshua never hesitated to obey when he clearly knew God's will, but there were rare occasions when Joshua's carelessness cost him and his people. One such event involved the Gibeonites, a Canaanite kingdom. God steadfastly prohibited the Israelites from making any treaties with the inhabitants of Canaan (Ex. 23:31–33; Deut. 7:1–5; 20:16–18). God warned His people that the Canaanites would become a spiritual snare to them if they were permitted to live among them. Joshua was well aware of this and never knowingly allowed a Canaanite to escape his sword.

The Gibeonites knew they could not defeat Joshua. The stories of God's mighty acts terrified them (Josh. 9:9–11, 24). While other kingdoms braced themselves for war with the invaders, the Gibeonites resorted to deceit. They sent emissaries who pretended to be from a distant country. The men convinced Joshua and the Israelite elders to sign a peace treaty with them (Josh. 9:1–27).

When the Israelites discovered that Joshua and the elders had been duped, they were justifiably upset (Josh. 9:18). This is the only scriptural reference to complaints against Joshua's leadership. Joshua had not knowingly disobeyed God. But could he have avoided this calamity?

When Joshua met the Gibeonite messengers, they showed him moldy bread, aged wineskins, and dusty sandals and clothes they claimed were new when they began their journey (Josh. 9:12–13). It appeared they had traveled much farther than from within the land of Canaan.

Joshua and the elders carefully inspected the evidence before them and concluded they were hearing the truth. However, "they did not ask counsel of the LORD" (Josh. 9:14). This was Joshua's sin. Perhaps buoyed by recent successes, he and the elders chose to use their own judgment and they failed to seek God's direction. They knew better. God had closely walked with them every step so far.

Perhaps the elders assumed that while they were clearly dependent on God to bring down fortress walls and to stop the flow of rivers, more straightforward tasks (such as interrogating foreign emissaries) were things they could handle on their own.

To Joshua's credit, he always learned from his mistakes. We do not read of another such lapse in his walk with God. As is the case with most sin, however, the consequences of even a momentary lapse can have lasting repercussions (2 Sam. 21:1–9). The Gibeonites remained in the promised land—a perpetual reminder of Joshua's oversight.

BIBLE CONTEMPLATION

> ### JOSHUA 9:14
> *"They did not ask counsel of the LORD."*

Is there a relationship or an experience in which you relied upon your own instincts instead of seeking the counsel of the Lord? What were the results?

_____

_____

_____

_____

UNIT 5—OBEDIENCE THAT GOES THE DISTANCE

Describe an experience in which God warned you, or someone you know, about a relationship and spared you from negative consequences.

_____

_____

_____

_____

Spiritual leaders are usually highly capable people. Joshua certainly was a bright and talented man. The temptation for such people is to rely on their own instincts and to call God in only for the big stuff. But over and over again the Bible warns against relying on one's own best thinking.

Surely Jesus was speaking to every generation when He said, "Without Me you can do nothing" (John 15:5). Wise leaders carefully consider what they are actually capable of accomplishing apart from God. The biblical answer, of course, is nothing.

BIBLE CONTEMPLATION

> ### JOHN 15:5
> *"I am the vine, you are the branches. He who abides in Me, and I in him, bears much fruit; for without Me you can do nothing."*

In what areas of your life do you tend to think you can make wise decisions without consulting or relying on God?

_____

_____

_____

_____

How could you guard against bypassing God's counsel?

_____

_____

_____

_____

Another Leader in God's Word

Samson: When Bad Things Keep Happening

Samson was one of the most famous judges in the history of Israel. Without a doubt, he was called and set apart by God for leadership. For years, he won great and mighty victories for the people of God through clever and powerful acts against the Philistines. The day came, however, when Samson made his own decisions rather than live in obedience to God. The result was a terrible defeat at the hands of Delilah and the lords of the Philistines. Judges 16:20 gives us this sad commentary on Samson's behavior: "He did not know that the LORD had departed from him."

One of the things a leader needs to consider when bad things keep happening in his life, work, or overall career, is this: "Has the Spirit of God departed?" Certainly those who have accepted Jesus Christ as their Savior have been given the Holy Spirit. The Holy Spirit does not depart completely from a genuine believer. But, the Holy Spirit can become so inactive in a person's life that it may seem as if the Spirit has departed. Too often people in leadership begin to blame other people or "circumstances" for their failures rather than face up to the fact that they may have allowed their relationship with God to become distant and cold, and as a result, they are no longer receiving God's full guidance and God's full blessing. If you are experiencing repeated failures at work . . . if a child is in full-blown rebellion . . . if relationships keep failing . . . if you are repeatedly fired from jobs . . . ask yourself, "How is my relationship with God?"

Before your relationships with others can ever be fully right, your relationship with God must be right. And right relationships are a key to successful leadership.

What might you do to turn around a setback or failure?

_____

_____

_____

Another Leader in God's Word

Ahab: Unteachable

A leader must always remain teachable. King Ahab was not. Although he was a brilliant administrator and a capable military commander, he disdained godly counsel. When he proposed to the godly King Jehoshaphat that they combine their armies to attack the Aramaeans, Jehoshaphat suggested they first seek the advice of counselors. Ahab summoned his foremost counselor, Zedekiah, who dutifully predicted what Ahab wanted to hear: complete victory. Jehoshaphat asked if there wasn't a prophet of the Lord that might be consulted. Ahab responded, "There is still one man by whom we may inquire of the LORD; but I hate him, because he never prophesies good concerning me, but always evil. He is Micaiah the son of Imla" (2 Chron. 18:7).

Sure enough, when Micaiah was called, he prophesied that Ahab's forces would be routed and Ahab slain. God warned Ahab through this prophet's words that if he proceeded with his plans, he would lose his life. How did Ahab respond? He threw the prophet in jail and marched off to battle. He refused to heed wise counsel and as a result, he died an ignoble death on a meaningless battlefield. The book of Proverbs tells us, "The fear of the LORD is the beginning of knowledge, but fools despise wisdom and instruction" (Prov. 1:7).

Reflect for a moment on the counsel that you have received about a difficult matter in your organization. Have you been told what your counselors know you want to hear? _____ Have you refused to heed negative counsel solely because it is negative and not what you want to do? _____ Is the negative counsel you have been given perhaps the wise counsel? Why or why not?

_____

_____

_____

CANAANITE SURVIVAL

Joshua's conquests were, on the whole, extremely extensive and successful. But there may have been another area where he was not as thorough as he should have been. While it appears that Joshua defeated many of his enemies, he did not defeat them all (Josh. 13:1–7). We read of his southern campaign:

And at that time Joshua came and cut off the Anakim from the mountains: from Hebron, from Debir, from Anab, from all the mountains of Judah, and from all the mountains of Israel; Joshua utterly destroyed them with their cities. None of the Anakim were left in the land of the children of Israel; they remained only in Gaza, in Gath, and in Ashdod. So Joshua took the whole land, according to all that the LORD had said to Moses; and Joshua gave it as an inheritance to Israel according to their divisions by their tribes. Then the land rested from war. (Joshua 11:21–23)

The Anakim were reportedly gigantic people (Num. 13:32–33). These were the mighty warriors who had petrified ten of the twelve spies. Joshua, however, appears to have defeated most of them. None were left in the lands occupied by the Israelites (Josh. 11:22). Yet they still resided in the outlying cities of Gaza, Gath, and Ashdod. These were cities God intended for the Israelites to ultimately conquer and inhabit. In fact, there were numerous regions left unconquered after Joshua laid down his sword (Judg. 1:27–2:6; 3:1–6).

Apparently Joshua had subdued the major cities and enemy fortresses throughout Canaan, but he left it to the individual tribes to complete the work of eradicating the enemy from the land. Most of the tribes failed to do this. The consequences were far-reaching.

Joshua failed to capture the city of Gath where the legendary Anakim lived. Gath became a Philistine stronghold that brought tremendous grief to the Israelites for generations. A champion Philistine soldier came out of Gath to humiliate the Israelites. His name was Goliath (1 Sam. 17:4). Later, the Philistines killed the Israelites' first king, Saul (1 Sam. 31). The inability of the Israelites to conquer the city of Gath as God intended cost their descendants dearly for many generations.

Joshua certainly was not willfully disobedient to God's command. He urged the people to complete the work he had begun. However, because Joshua's generation failed to completely remove the Canaanites from the land, the Israelites were soon tempted by the pagan practices and loose morals of their Canaanite neighbors, just as God had predicted (Judg. 2:11–15; 3:7). This would bring enormous suffering and grief to Israel until their disloyalty ultimately cost them four hundred years of turmoil during the period of the judges and later seventy years of exile in Babylon.

PERSONAL RESPONSE

How is a partial completion of God's instructions a failure?

_____

_____

_____

What is required for a person or group to remain motivated to completely fulfill God's commands?

_____

_____

_____

UNIT 5—OBEDIENCE THAT GOES THE DISTANCE

TAKING GOD'S ORDERS SERIOUSLY

Joshua was not perfect in his walk with God. There were times when he failed to complete everything God instructed. Yet throughout his life, Joshua took God's instructions extremely seriously. Joshua saw God's word as wholly binding upon him. With Joshua there was no quarreling. There was no negotiating. There was no delaying. There was no revising. There was only absolute and immediate obedience. Such an attitude was the key to his success.

UNIT 6

CHARACTER: THE FOUNDATION FOR LEADERSHIP

> *Then Joshua gathered all the tribes of Israel to Shechem and called for the elders of Israel, for their heads, for their judges, and for their officers; and they presented themselves before God. And Joshua said to all the people . . .*
>
> *"Now therefore, fear the LORD, serve Him in sincerity and in truth, and put away the gods which your fathers served on the other side of the River and in Egypt. Serve the LORD! And if it seems evil to you to serve the LORD, choose for yourselves this day whom you will serve, whether the gods which your fathers served that were on the other side of the River, or the gods of the Amorites, in whose land you dwell. But as for me and my house, we will serve the LORD."*
>
> JOSHUA 24:1–2, 14–15

The common denominator among all those God used mightily is character. That is not to say each of these people had "arrived" and attained perfection. But they were all willing for God to shape them and stretch them into the people He needed for His assignments. That potential, which lay deep within—so deep that sometimes only God could see it—was their character.

DAY ONE

CHARACTER: THE KEY TO SUCCESS

It seems somewhat unusual that the biblical account of a mighty general like Joshua makes no mention of his size or strength or appearance. In an age where brawn counted for a lot, Joshua's physical features seemed irrelevant. In God's kingdom such things don't matter; character does. People can only do so much to improve their physical and mental abilities, but the potential for character growth is limitless.

Big assignments require a certain maturity of character. Biblically, when God had an important task, He usually bypassed the most obvious candidates (according to the world's perspective). He chose a poor, unknown teenage girl to bear the Messiah. He chose a simple shepherd boy to be Israel's greatest king. He called on an outspoken, impulsive fisherman to become an apostle.

CONCEPT REFLECTION

CONCEPT: People can only do so much to improve their physical and mental abilities, but the potential for character growth is limitless.

What is your response to the concept that your potential for character development is limitless?

_____

_____

_____

Do you believe a person is responsible for his or her own character? _____
Partially or totally? _____ Why?

_____

_____

_____

Joshua's case is somewhat unusual for a leader who is mentioned so often in the Bible. Invariably a spiritual leader, no matter how famous, will eventually reveal a character flaw. But Joshua doesn't. This doesn't mean he was sinless but that he had no character weakness significant enough for Scripture to mention.

- Noah was the only righteous man on earth, but he still became drunk with wine and disgraced himself (Gen. 9:21).

- Abraham was a man of faith, but he was also a liar (Gen. 12:11–13; 20:2).

- Abraham's son Isaac was a liar, and Isaac's son Jacob was a deceiver (Gen. 26:7; 27:19).

- Moses struggled with anger (Ex. 2:11–12; 32:19; Num. 20:1–13; Lev. 10:16).

- King Saul was jealous, and King David was adulterous (1 Sam. 18:7–9; 2 Sam. 11:4).

History's most celebrated leaders have been plagued by every besetting sin imaginable; these pages are not extensive enough to chronicle them.

PERSONAL RESPONSE

Is there a character trait you desire to change or strengthen? _____
What could you do to see the results you desire?

_____

_____

_____

Is there a habit you desire to change or a strength you would like to acquire?
_____ What could you do to achieve the results you desire?

_____

_____

_____

What is the link between character traits and habits?

_____

_____

_____

What people do spontaneously or when no one is watching reveals their character. Likewise, what people do habitually reflects what lies within them. A leader's skills can temporarily mask a weak character, but eventually all leaders are revealed for who they really are. A charming, charismatic person may fool people for a time, but inevitably a lack of Christlike character becomes apparent (Matt. 7:15–20).

King Saul was Israel's first monarch. The Israelites craved someone who looked like the kings of other nations. They clamored for a leader who could carry himself with pomp and splendor like the world's great monarchs (1 Sam. 8:19–20). So God gave them a man who had all the qualities important to them. He was tall and physically impressive. He could act like a king, and he demanded his people's respect.

After King Saul's coronation, his shallow character quickly showed itself.

For one thing, he could be greedy (1 Sam. 15:9). He made harsh, unreasonable demands of his people. He was even prepared to execute his own son for disobeying his foolish orders (1 Sam. 14:44). Yet he showed no compunction in breaking God's laws (1 Sam. 13:13; 15:19).

As time wore on, Saul revealed a petty jealousy of anyone who threatened his position (1 Sam. 18:8). Though a king, Saul was even jealous of his servant (1 Sam. 18:12). Saul's character was marked by paranoia, self-pity, and cruel vengeance (1 Sam. 22:8, 17–18). Even when David twice spared his life, Saul's unrelenting hatred drove him to doggedly pursue David and his men (1 Sam. 24:16–22; 26:21–25).

Saul's life is a tragic illustration of the difference between charisma and character. He appeared impressive on the outside but the longer he ruled, the more obvious it became that his character was not robust enough to sustain his position. It is a dangerous venture to hold a position that is larger than your character.

PERSONAL RESPONSE

In your own words, define the difference between charisma and character:

_____

_____

_____

Joshua's life exemplifies the qualities of a genuine leader. Joshua didn't obtain his position overnight as Saul did, but when he eventually achieved it, he was ready for it. Joshua never took on more than he could handle. His success never inflated his ego. He never seemed overwhelmed by his responsibilities. His character always matched the challenge that lay before him. When God chooses a leader He doesn't bypass character. He develops those He calls into people of moral strength. Then He uses them as His servants to build His kingdom.

Unfortunately, churches often place more value on charisma than on character. They select pastors who look impressive and who make a good first impression, but they are later disappointed when their pastor's true character comes to light. Men and women are given important leadership roles because of their attractive appearance or prominent position or financial status rather than because of their close walk with God. It is not the godliest church members who clamor for positions and recognition. As a result they are often bypassed while people of lesser integrity assume roles that don't suit their character.

Was Joshua perfect when God chose him? Of course not. But he was will-

When God chooses a leader He doesn't bypass character.

UNIT 6—CHARACTER: THE FOUNDATION FOR LEADERSHIP

ing for God to strengthen him and to work into him the godly qualities necessary for the enormous assignment of leading a nation. Saul, on the other hand, seems to have degenerated the longer he remained in power. His character simply couldn't handle the burden of leadership. Joshua paid the price to be the man God wanted him to be. Saul didn't earn his position, so he never developed the strength of character to maintain it.

PERSONAL RESPONSE

How is earning a position important to both character development and leadership success?

_____

_____

_____

_____

DAY TWO

CHARACTER: FORGED BY CRISIS

One might assume Joshua's greatness came not just from the hardship of his early life but also from the challenges of a difficult adulthood. He was beset by one painful, disappointing experience after another.

He was born into slavery. It would seem he lost his parents at a relatively early age. He spent forty years in a wilderness because his colleagues lacked faith. He watched his spiritual leaders and heroes die one by one until only the grizzled Caleb remained. Even when Joshua was experiencing success as his nation's preeminent general, he was immersed in constant warfare and bloodshed. His was not an easy life.

Joshua could not pick and choose God's assignments for him. He had no control over what his fellow Israelites or his enemies would do. What Joshua could determine was how accessible to God his life would be. Regardless of whether God allowed Joshua to enter the promised land or not, Joshua could experience God working in his own life.

Whether or not Joshua ever saw the land of Canaan transformed into a dwelling place for God's people, he could experience God transforming his character into one that glorified God. A person's character is the sphere in which God delights to work. God receives glory through a godly character.

PERSONAL RESPONSE

How can you allow God to have access to all areas of your life?

_____

_____

_____

What limitations or barriers are you likely to put in place?

_____

_____

_____

A strong character never happens overnight. It always involves more than simply gaining knowledge of God's Word. It takes living out the truth of God's Word in real-life situations.

A weak, underdeveloped character is no match for the spiritual magnitude of leading God's people. It is crucial for a leader that God builds his or her character. This always comes at a cost. Usually the process begins when the leader is young. Such was the case in both Moses' and Joshua's lives.

PERSONAL RESPONSE

What are the key differences between knowledge of God's Word and living out the truth of God's Word?

_____

_____

_____

_____

Many of the character traits that run deepest are those that are driven in hardest. Hard times imprint themselves into a person's character. Trials either leave a scar of bitterness and cynicism, or they forge strength, humility, and compassion.

CONCEPT REFLECTION

CONCEPT: **Trials either leave a scar of bitterness and cynicism, or they forge strength, humility, and compassion.**

A weak, underdeveloped character is no match for the spiritual magnitude of leading God's people.

Trials either leave a scar of bitterness and cynicism, or they forge strength, humility, and compassion.

Identify an instance in which you have witnessed the impact that a personal hardship or trial had on a person's character: _____
How did the person's response to the trial impact his or her future?

_____

_____

_____

_____

The difference is wholly dependent upon how people respond to their life situations and, more important, how they respond to God in the midst of those circumstances (Rom. 8:28). While no one but a masochist looks for opportunities to suffer, people who truly desire to be Christlike in every part of their lives will welcome whatever instrument God uses to make them so.

It was James who urged believers to "count it all joy when you fall into various trials, knowing that the testing of your faith produces patience. But let patience have its perfect work, that you may be perfect and complete, lacking nothing" (James 1:2–4).

BIBLE CONTEMPLATION

JAMES 1:2–4

"My brethren, count it all joy when you fall into various trials, knowing that the testing of your faith produces patience. But let patience have its perfect work, that you may be perfect and complete, lacking nothing."

What do you believe is the "perfect work" of patience?

_____

_____

_____

_____

Joshua approached the challenging moments of his life with great faith and humble dependence on God. While hardships tempted many of his colleagues to forfeit their faith, Joshua grew to trust God more. The result was a sterling moral fiber that could stand firm in the face of temptation, fear, and doubt.

Added Insight into Spiritual Leadership

The Time It Takes

Two factors determine the length of time required for God to develop character worthy of spiritual leadership—trust in God and obedience to God.

Recall an experience or incident in your life in which you learned the great importance of trusting God—perhaps trusting God for results that seemed unlikely from a human perspective, trusting Him when it came to timing that seemed unusual or risky, or trusting Him as He led you to use a particular method that seemed unconventional:

_____

_____

_____

Recall an experience in which you learned the great importance of obeying God *fully:*

_____

_____

_____

DAY THREE

Character: Keeping Your Word

Joshua was a man of his word. There was always a perfect match between his words and his actions. When he sent two spies to reconnoiter Jericho, the local authorities attempted to arrest them. Only the intervention of Rahab, the harlot, saved their lives (Josh. 2). In response to her kindness, the two spies promised to spare her and any of her family members who gathered in her home during the upcoming attack.

On the day of the assault, Joshua saw to it that this promise was honored (Josh. 6:17, 22–25). In Joshua's day, men did not normally enter into agreements with women. Certainly a promise to a prostitute could have been excused or forgotten during the intensity of battle. Joshua had not even made the promise himself, but he was diligent to keep it.

PERSONAL RESPONSE

Do you believe a leader is responsible for fulfilling the promises made by his or her subordinates? To what extent?

_____

_____

_____

By his or her predecessors? To what extent?

_____

_____

_____

When Joshua and the elders were duped by the Gibeonites, they promised to enter into a peace treaty with them. After the Israelites discovered the deception, their first impulse was to immediately destroy their clever enemy. Nevertheless, Joshua and the elders chose to honor their word (Josh. 9:17–19). Even though they had been outmaneuvered, Joshua and his colleagues believed they would be accountable to God for not keeping their promise. Such fidelity to one's word is truly remarkable.

PERSONAL RESPONSE

What do you think is the foremost reason(s) for a person's failiureto keep his word?

_____

_____

_____

Does God allow any of these reasons as excuses?_____

Joshua's stalwart adherence to his word brought him great respect. When Joshua had Achan put to death for disobeying God, he vowed to do the same to the next person caught violating God's commands. Everyone knew he meant it. Joshua never deceived them. He never retracted his words. To know what Joshua said was to know what he would do. This gave his followers tremendous confidence.

A sure way for a leader to forfeit his influence with followers is to make careless promises. Some leaders enter organizations effusing promises to all who listen. Every good idea that enters their heads becomes a promise from their lips. Yet as quickly as the oaths are out of their mouths, they are just as readily forgotten. Followers soon recognize such people and grow to disregard everything they say.

PERSONAL RESPONSE

How does a leader's following through on promises instill confidence in his or her followers?

_____

_____

_____

How does a leader's refusal to make rash promises instill confidence in his or her followers?

_____

_____

_____

How does a leader's making rash threats undermine confidence in his or her followers?

_____

_____

_____

Some leaders repeatedly threaten to resign if they do not get their way, but they never follow through. Others promise to listen to any suggestion, but they become angry and defensive when critiqued. Others promise to faithfully support their colleagues, but they disappear when the pressure is on.

Some of the most haphazard vows made are those offered to God. It is sobering to consider how many empty promises God hears from well-intentioned but insincere people. Scripture warns of the gravity of not keeping vows made to God (Eccl. 5:2–5). Leaders' words are their currency, but those words are worthless unless they are backed by action.

CHARACTER: KEEPING YOUR HEAD

Certainly no Israelite was more highly esteemed in his day than Joshua. Scripture indicates, "The LORD exalted Joshua in the sight of all Israel; and they feared him, as they had feared Moses, all the days of his life . . . so the LORD was with Joshua, and his fame spread throughout all the country" (Josh. 4:14; 6:27).

Surely such honor from God and such respect by the people would have provided ample opportunity for Joshua to gain a high opinion of himself. Yet despite reaching the pinnacle of military and political power, Joshua never allowed his success to go to his head. He remained God's faithful servant throughout his life.

Joshua was meticulous in giving God the credit for his success. He continually reminded people that it was not his military stratagems or brilliant feats on the battlefield that brought victory. Rather he steadfastly pointed to God's presence as the key:

And Joshua said to the people, "Sanctify yourselves, for tomorrow the LORD will do wonders among you." (Joshua 3:5)

For the LORD your God dried up the waters of the Jordan before you until you had crossed over, as the LORD your God did to the Red Sea, which He dried up before us until we had crossed over. (Joshua 4:23)

You have seen all that the LORD your God has done to all these nations because of you, for the LORD your God is He who has fought for you. (Joshua 23:3)

For the LORD our God is He who brought us and our fathers up out of the land of Egypt, from the house of bondage, who did those great signs in our sight, and preserved us in all the way that we went and among all the people through whom we passed. (Joshua 24:17)

Joshua could easily have assumed he was at least *partially* responsible for the Israelites' dramatic success, but he didn't. Today's Christian leaders struggle with how to view their careers. Successful businessmen who have amassed fortunes through wise business practices and prudent investments can assume that while God has blessed them (whatever that means), their success came by their own diligence and shrewdness. Pastors of growing churches can conclude that the development of their church is due in large part to their own leadership skills and the passionate vision they have pursued for their congregations.

However, Joshua understood that ultimately, nothing he did had significance unless God affirmed it. God gave Joshua every skill and every strategy he brought to the battlefield, because God was the author of Joshua's very life.

PERSONAL RESPONSE

Is it possible for a person to have lasting significance or lasting success without God's affirmation? How? If it is not possible, give reasons why not.

_____

_____

_____

What does it mean to keep success in proper perspective?

_____

_____

_____

How does a person do this?

_____

_____

_____

ADDED INSIGHT INTO SPIRITUAL LEADERSHIP

PROCESSING THE SUCCESS

A wise leader will take time to process successes. Many times, leaders focus mostly on problems. Don't we tend to do a lot more Monday-morning quarterbacking after a loss than a win? Take time to analyze why a success is a success. After the great miracle in which Jesus fed five thousand families from a little boy's lunch of a few fishes and loaves, Jesus immediately went apart from the crowds to spend time alone with His heavenly Father. He "departed to the

UNIT 6—CHARACTER: THE FOUNDATION FOR LEADERSHIP

mountain to pray" (Mark 6:46). In His frequent encounters with the Father—morning and nightly prayer times—Jesus kept His balance and never strayed from the Father's plan and agenda for His life.

In contrast, the disciples of Jesus seem to have done far less processing of the miracles they witnessed. The Bible tells us that in the aftermath of the same miracle, the disciples "had not understood about the loaves, because their heart was hardened" (Mark 6:52).

When you take time to process a success, you generally come to the conclusion that absolute obedience to God's plan and agenda is a must. You are likely to come to other conclusions as well, such as: God's grace is abundant, God's ways are higher than man's ways, God's results are more than we can ask or imagine. You are also likely to be drawn to the conclusions: hard work is good, but hard work alone doesn't produce success; the help of others is vital, but the sovereign work of God is what makes the difference; a good environment and business climate are helpful, but the presence of God is indispensable (Eph. 3:20–21).

Identify a recent success you have experienced. Take time to analyze it. What aspects of your success do you need to remember and apply to your next endeavor?

_____

_____

_____

_____

Joshua's dismal experience at the city of Ai was proof enough, if he needed any, that God's presence was everything. The moment God withdrew His presence from the previously undefeated Israelite forces, their army was turned back in a rout.

We counsel numerous Christian CEOs of large corporations. When we ask why they believe they have achieved so much, many give a sober reply. They cannot always explain why they have enjoyed such prosperity. They have friends who've worked as hard and who have more talent, yet their colleagues have not fared as well.

It becomes apparent that despite their strenuous efforts, their success has caught them by surprise. Often they conclude God must want to use them for some purpose and that's why He has allowed them to succeed. We know many CEOs and business owners who take their faith seriously and make significant sacrifices so that their companies honor God.

Several Christian business owners have refused to downsize their companies when the economy plummeted, even though it would have been seen as a prudent step to take. As a result, they spared hundreds of families from financial hardship.

The founder of a software company established a charitable foundation with a portion of his earnings and used it to promote Christian education around the world. A businesswoman used her personal resources to found and fund an orphanage in an impoverished region in Asia. Owners of professional sports teams have hired chaplains to help players find Christ and then to disciple them. Some CEOs give of their personal wealth to provide aid to the poor or to sponsor mission projects such as building houses for impoverished families. Others have used their influential positions to pressure television networks to remove morally offensive advertisements during family viewing hours.

Some Christian business leaders use their private jets to transport church leaders to ministry events. Many offer their vacation properties as places of restful retreat for overwhelmed Christian ministers and their families. Some use their wealth to start up Christian enterprises or to have Christian materials published and distributed.

Many CEOs generously invest company resources to help employees further their education and skill development. Some business owners invest their resources in providing Christian counseling to employees. Some corporate executives use their access to world leaders as an opportunity to share the gospel with the world's most powerful people.

The list of ways Christian business leaders have invested their influence and wealth in the kingdom of God seems endless. These practices do not always seem to make the best business sense, but these Christian leaders know it is one way God is using them to build *His* kingdom.

These leaders (and we haven't named them) don't do this to win accolades, but we can assure you that throughout the corporate world, there are many fine Christian leaders who are making a profound difference in those they lead. They are doing it because they understand that their success is really God's success.

PERSONAL RESPONSE

How is God leading you to use your success for the furthering of His purposes?

_____

_____

_____

When Christian business leaders assume they are the authors of their own success, they lack a sense of divine stewardship. Their focus is on amassing their fortune rather than building God's kingdom. They achieve personal glory rather than glorifying God. They write "how to" books so that people can copy their success, but they don't point people to God.

Some Christian businesspeople live the first half of their lives feverishly gaining fame and fortune by their own efforts. Then, once they have achieved their goals and obtained a comfortable level of wealth, they turn to God and unconvincingly give the glory to God for their accomplishments. Biblically, however, this does not honor God. That is merely second-hand glory, and God does not take second place in anyone's life. God does not receive glory by making *our* plans succeed, but by accomplishing *His* will. Joshua understood this. From the outset of his military career until his retirement speech, Joshua regularly and sincerely gave all the glory to God for his success. In his mind, it *was* God's success.

PERSONAL RESPONSE

What do you believe to be a godly use of success, power, fame, or fortune?

_____

_____

_____

_____

God does not take second place in anyone's life. God does not receive glory by making our plans succeed, but by accomplishing His will.

CONCEPT REFLECTION

CONCEPT: **God does not receive glory by making *our* plans succeed, but by accomplishing *His* will.**

What criteria could a person use to evaluate whether he or she is pursuing achievement for *personal* glory instead of *God's* glory?

_____

_____

_____

A sure way to tell what people are made of is to examine what they do with success and the accompanying power and fame it brings. Joshua could have brokered his exalted position to benefit himself financially, but he never abused the office God entrusted to him. After accomplishing God's assignment, he voluntarily stepped down and out of the limelight.

Joshua did not need a prestigious job to feel significant. He did not derive his self-worth from the attention and praise of others. He did not nurse feelings of entitlement as a result of his labors. His relationship with God gave him more than enough reason to feel satisfied.

Joshua was surrounded by success and power. Kings paid homage to him. Yet Joshua kept his feet on the ground and never allowed his success to go to his head.

ANOTHER LEADER IN GOD'S WORD

PAUL: AN ANTICIPATED REWARD

At the end of his life, the apostle Paul wrote, "I have fought the good fight, I have finished the race, I have kept the faith. Finally, there is laid up for me the crown of righteousness, which the Lord, the righteous Judge, will give to me on that Day, and not to me only but also to all who have loved His appearing" (2 Tim. 4:7–8). Paul anticipated the true reward for a spiritual leader who has led well. Paul knew that worldly prestige and honors were incomparable to pleasing God, who had given him his leadership position in the first place.

If the Lord called you in today for an evaluation meeting about your leadership, what do you believe would be His comments to you about the job you are doing and have done?

_____

_____

_____

What might you do to improve your evaluation?

_____

_____

_____

DAY FIVE

CHARACTER: CONSIDERING OTHERS

It has been said, "No man is a hero to his valet." Peruse the biography section of a bookstore and notice how many former employees and attendants enthusiastically reveal the scandalous side of their famous former employers. Many widely acclaimed heroes and admired leaders are not looked upon so highly by those who must work with them on a daily basis.

God exalted Joshua before his people. It would have been easy for him to abuse this influence over others. Joshua never believed that because he had accomplished much for his people he was entitled to any special favors or honors. There is no evidence that Joshua's success desensitized him to those he led. There is no record of Joshua being self-centered. By all accounts Joshua's people willingly followed him anywhere and faced any enemy.

When Joshua was dividing the promised land among the tribes and families of Israel, he had everyone else receive their inheritance before he was finally given his own plot (Josh. 19:49–51). No one had worked harder or played a more decisive role in the Israelites' success than Joshua. But he was the last to benefit personally from his own victories, and he received no more than anyone else. Obviously Joshua was a humble man of integrity who knew who he was and to whom he was accountable.

There is no evidence that Joshua's success desensitized him to those he led.

PERSONAL RESPONSE

To whom are you accountable? _____ Does this answer apply to all areas of your life? Why or why not?

_____

_____

_____

Three marks of great leaders are:

1. They are sensitive to the needs of those they lead.

2. They treat their enemies with dignity and grace.

3. They conduct themselves with humility—which doesn't demand respect or pursue revenge. Humility only seeks a "well done" from the Lord.

PERSONAL RESPONSE

In what ways might you become more sensitive to the needs of those you lead?

_____

_____

_____

Humility doesn't demand respect or pursue revenge; humility only seeks a "well done" from the Lord.

In what practical ways might you treat your enemies with dignity and grace?

_____

_____

_____

CHARACTER: ACCOUNTABLE TO GOD

Having a Christlike character is possible for every believer; God can do a transforming work in any person who is willing to let Him. But He leaves the choice to us. At the close of his life, Joshua urged the Israelites to "hold fast to the LORD" (Josh. 23:8). Joshua had spent a lifetime choosing God's way. Sometimes it meant risking his reputation. God often told him to do things that went against commonly accepted military and administrative opinion. Imagine announcing to your military officers God's plan for taking down the walls of Jericho! Joshua often faced the prospect of ridicule and second-guessing from those he led, yet he chose to cling to the Lord.

Joshua challenged the people to "choose for yourselves this day whom you will serve." Then he declared his own allegiance, and his words have become a mantra for believers ever since: "As for me and my house, we will serve the LORD" (Josh. 24:15).

Every person has the same option. It makes no difference whether one has been raised in a Christian environment or in an atheist household, whether a person is highly educated or illiterate, wealthy or destitute; choosing to obey God is a conscious decision every person has to regularly make.

PERSONAL RESPONSE

In what way(s) have you—or _could_ you—let your followers know about your relationship with and reliance on God?

_____

_____

_____

In what way(s) have you—or _could_ you—challenge your followers to make a choice for the Lord?

_____

_____

_____

Is there any time or situation in which it is God's wisdom to remain silent about your relationship with, reliance on, or choice for the Lord?

_____

_____

_____

Joshua clarified why he was so careful to obey God: "He is a holy God. He is a jealous God . . . If you forsake the LORD and serve foreign gods, then He will turn and do you harm and consume you, after He has done you good" (Josh. 24:19–20). Joshua knew he could not serve a holy God with an unholy life. Knowing what God was like gave Joshua the proper perspective to dutifully serve his Lord.

It wasn't a question of feelings or rights or preferences. It was a matter of reverence. Out of his awe for God grew a keen sense of accountability. Joshua realized God would discipline him if he abandoned His divine covenant. Knowing this, Joshua's only option was to completely submit himself to God. At the root of Joshua's faithfulness was a healthy fear of the Lord. He exhorted his people: "Fear the LORD, serve Him in sincerity and in truth" (Josh. 24:14).

> **It wasn't a question of feelings or rights or preferences. It was a matter of reverence.**

BIBLE CONTEMPLATION

> ### JOSHUA 24:14
> *"Fear the LORD, serve Him in sincerity and in truth."*

What are some practical ways to do this in today's world?

_____

_____

_____

Without exception, great spiritual leaders have a profound sense of accountability. They are guided by the realization that no matter how highly esteemed they are by people in this life, one day they will stand before almighty God. They will be face-to-face with their Creator and their lives will be completely exposed for what they are, merits and faults alike. This truth terrified the apostle Paul. He knew full well the "terror of the Lord." He was constantly aware that serving God was serious business:

> **Without exception, great spiritual leaders have a profound sense of accountability.**

Therefore we make it our aim, whether present or absent, to be well pleasing to Him. For we must all appear before the judgment seat of Christ, that each one may receive the things done in the body, according to what he has done, whether good or bad. Knowing, therefore, the terror of the Lord, we persuade men; but we are well known to God. (2 Corinthians 5:9–11)

Tragically, many Christian leaders today are devoid of a profound sense of reverence for God. Today's Christian culture so emphasizes God's unmerited love, that to mention God's holiness and judgment is considered poor taste. Yet the writer of Proverbs urges wise people to maintain a palpable fear and reverence for God:

> Then you will understand the fear of the LORD,
> And find the knowledge of God. (Proverbs 2:5)

> Do not be wise in your own eyes;
> Fear the LORD and depart from evil. (Proverbs 3:7)

> The fear of the LORD prolongs days,
> But the years of the wicked will be shortened. (Proverbs 10:27)

> The fear of the LORD leads to life,
> And he who has it will abide in satisfaction;
> He will not be visited with evil. (Proverbs 19:23)

PERSONAL RESPONSE

What does it mean to have a profound sense of reverence for God?

It is impossible to fear God and yet tolerate sin in your life.

It is impossible to fear God and yet tolerate sin in your life. Sin takes on an entirely different look when you are keenly aware you will one day give an account for it! God declares Himself to be a jealous God. This truth should profoundly impact those who follow Him. It is incredible that almighty God cares what His creatures do or believe. It is a costly mistake for people to assume God is either too distant to know what they are doing or too far removed in majesty to care about their loyalty or affections.

Joshua, the inveterate warrior, understood that God coveted his allegiance. God would not look the other way if Joshua betrayed Him. God would never be satisfied with the crumbs that fell from the plate of Joshua's affections.

UNIT 6—CHARACTER: THE FOUNDATION FOR LEADERSHIP

Joshua urged people to either wholeheartedly follow God or reject Him. He discouraged them from trying to follow God in a lackadaisical fashion. This, God would never accept (Josh. 24:19–20).

PERSONAL RESPONSE

In what ways might you be tolerating sin in your life?

_____

_____

_____

What does God desire?

_____

_____

_____

NO SHORTCUTS

There are no shortcuts to success with God. God will systematically and thoroughly work *in* you as He works *through* you, because God is seeking to do far more through your life than you could imagine. He is constantly stretching you and molding you and fashioning your character to be like Christ's. The deeper your walk with God, the more Christlike your character will be. Wholly submitting yourself to God's will is the surest way to have a life God is pleased to use for His purposes.

ADDED INSIGHT INTO SPIRITUAL LEADERSHIP

ACCOUNTABLE TO GOD

Perhaps the most sobering realization a leader can ever have is that he or she must one day give an account to God for every decision they make. Leaders are not accountable to their followers, their clients, their customers, their shareholders, government agencies, the public at large, or even to themselves, as much as they are accountable to God. It is God who raises up a person into leadership. It is to God that a leader is accountable.

Paul wrote, "We make it our aim, whether present or absent, to be well pleasing to Him. For we must all appear before the judgment seat of Christ, that each one may receive the things done in the body, according to what he has done, whether good or bad" (2 Cor. 5:9–10). Paul enjoyed a close relationship with Christ, yet he knew the awesome God he served. He admonished his followers that they *all* would be accountable to the risen Christ for their actions.

In what ways might you more diligently remember that *all* of your decisions as a spiritual leader are subject to God's scrutiny and evaluation?

_____

_____

_____

FAITH THAT BRINGS WALLS DOWN

> [The LORD spoke to Joshua,] "Be strong and of good courage, for to this people you shall divide as an inheritance the land which I swore to their fathers to give them. Only be strong and very courageous, that you may observe to do according to all the law which Moses My servant commanded you . . . Have I not commanded you? Be strong and of good courage; do not be afraid, nor be dismayed, for the LORD your God is with you wherever you go."
>
> JOSHUA 1:6–7, 9

Scripture says, "Faith is the substance of things hoped for, the evidence of things not seen . . . But without faith it is impossible to please Him" (Heb. 11:1, 6). Faith means trusting God regardless of your circumstances. Faith means looking beyond the current situation and believing God will keep His promises. History's greatest saints have been ordinary people who held tenaciously to God's Word no matter what they encountered. God profoundly rewards those who put their faith in Him and leave it there.

Joshua's life was characterized by indomitable faith. He did not base his trust on life events but on his firsthand knowledge of God. Joshua's unshakable confidence in God becomes obvious as you examine the way he lived his life.

History's greatest saints have been ordinary people who held tenaciously to God's Word no matter what they encountered.

DAY ONE

FAITH THAT STANDS FIRM

Leading followers is one thing. Leading leaders is another. When spies were needed to investigate Canaan, each of the twelve tribes chose a prominent leader to represent them. Joshua was honored to be among them (Num. 13:2). Modern Bible teachers sometimes portray ten of these men as cowardly wimps. This is unquestionably too harsh. Each of these soldiers had risen to the apex

Leading followers is one thing. Leading leaders is another.

of leadership in his tribe. Out of tribes consisting of tens of thousands, each was perceived as a strong, dominant leader. These men were respected. They were trusted. They had already proved themselves to be capable leaders, so when they spoke, people listened.

This band of spies spent forty days together while surveying Canaan. They traveled together; they ate their meals together; they hid from enemy patrols together. At night they took turns standing watch to protect each other. They undoubtedly had strong personalities and fervent opinions. Joshua may have been one of the youngest men on this dangerous mission. Day after day Joshua would have listened to his persuasive comrades vehemently argue their views about the feasibility of conquering Canaan.

When the group returned to report to their kinsmen, it was a pivotal moment in Israel's history. Ten of the spies began by describing a fertile and prosperous land, rich in resources. Then their account turned negative. They spoke of fierce giants and fortified cities (Num. 13:28–29, 31–33). These reputable men were doing exactly what they had been asked to do—reporting on what they saw.

As these eloquent spokesmen warmed to their subject, the people grew increasingly terrified. Obviously they were convincing. No one from the crowd challenged their opinion. No one questioned their information. No one charged them with cowardice. The testimony from such respected leaders sent an entire nation into a state of unrestrained pandemonium. Even Moses and Aaron fell on their faces before the people. Then it was Joshua's turn.

What was Joshua to do? These men were passionate. They were convincing. They had the nation's attention and their trust. To speak out against such popular leaders would take enormous courage. Besides, Joshua could not dispute the facts. There *were* fierce enemies. There *were* strong, fortified cities.

Joshua and the ten reluctant spies were looking at the same situation, but from different perspectives. Here is the report Joshua and Caleb gave:

> The land we passed through to spy out is an exceedingly good land. If the LORD delights in us, then He will bring us into this land and give it to us, "a land which flows with milk and honey." Only do not rebel against the LORD, nor fear the people of the land, for they are our bread; their protection has departed from them, and the LORD is with us. Do not fear them. (Numbers 14:7–9)

It was not a popular opinion to be shared at that moment! In fact, the people prepared to stone Joshua and Caleb to silence them (Num. 14:10). How much courage does it take to look in the faces of thousands of terrified people and tell them their viewpoint is wrong—that their fear is misplaced? What temerity is required to publicly disagree with ten of the nation's most trusted leaders?

UNIT 7—FAITH THAT BRINGS WALLS DOWN

What kind of character is required to face a hostile and murderous mob, yet to tenaciously hold firm to one's convictions?

PERSONAL RESPONSE

What do you believe gives a leader courage to go against popular opinion, peer pressure, or powerful and persuasive people?

_____

_____

_____

Joshua had faith. He knew God. He knew, regardless of his enemies' size or strength, and no matter how weak he felt, with God all things were possible. It wasn't a matter of what Joshua did _not_ know. His faith was based on what he _did_ know. At this point Joshua faced a number of unknowns: He had no idea how many enemy soldiers his army would face. He could not anticipate his opponents' resources and alliances. Neither was he aware of God's plan to hold the sun in its place or to topple city walls. But he knew God, and everything he knew about God assured him he had nothing to fear.

Joshua's faith was not based on public opinion or on his own resources. It came out of his experiential knowledge of God. It was not a blind faith but faith based on his personal experience with God. After all, had God not already delivered them from Egypt and brought them safely to this moment? All twelve spies had the same evidence. But Joshua had a practical faith in God, and this made all the difference.

It wasn't a matter of what Joshua did _not_ know. His faith was based on what he _did_ know.

CONCEPT REFLECTION

CONCEPT: **Joshua's faith was based on what he did know.**

What do you know about God with rock-solid confidence and assurance?

_____

_____

_____

Joshua knew that as long as he had received a promise from God, there was no reason to fret over the details. God would provide. He chose to focus on God and His Word rather than on the problems and the unknowns. Even when

Even when obstacles immobilized most of the people around him, Joshua was motivated by the God he knew.

obstacles immobilized most of the people around him, Joshua was motivated by the God he knew. That is not to imply a careless disregard for the difficult task ahead. Joshua was a skilled and competent leader in every respect.

PERSONAL RESPONSE

What are some of the factors that help a person focus on God and His Word rather than on problems and unknowns?

_____

_____

_____

_____

_____

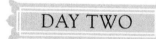

DAY TWO

FAITH: ONE STEP AT A TIME

The first logistical problem Joshua faced was the Jordan River. It was a formidable barrier, especially during flood season when the melting snows from the northern mountains could expand the floodplain up to a mile wide. During that time the flowing waters were transformed into a raging torrent. It would be an organizational nightmare to transport the supplies and equipment for an entire nation across the swollen river. God had previously performed a great miracle during Moses' leadership when He parted the Red Sea. The people had not yet seen if God would work as powerfully through Joshua. God parted a sea for Moses; would He stem a river's flow for Joshua?

We are not told if Joshua's faith wavered during his first big test, but his conduct indicates a steadfast trust in God:

So Joshua said to the children of Israel, "Come here, and hear the words of the LORD your God." And Joshua said, "By this you shall know that the living God is among you, and that He will without fail drive out from before you the Canaanites and the Hittites and the Hivites and the Perizzites and the Girgashites and the Amorites and the Jebusites: Behold, the ark of the covenant of the Lord of all the earth is crossing over before you into the Jordan. Now therefore, take for yourselves twelve men from the tribes of Israel, one man from every tribe. And it shall come to pass, as soon as the soles of the feet of the priests who bear the ark of the LORD, the Lord of all the earth, shall rest in the waters of the Jordan, that the waters of the Jordan shall be cut off, the waters that come down from upstream, and they shall stand as a heap." So it was, when the people set out from their camp to cross over the Jordan, with the priests bearing the ark of the covenant before the people, and as those who bore the ark came to the Jordan, and the feet of the priests who bore the ark dipped in the edge of the water (for the Jordan overflows all its banks during the whole time of harvest), that the waters which came down from upstream stood still, and rose in a heap very far away at Adam, the city that is beside Zaretan. So the waters that went down into the Sea of the Arabah, the Salt Sea, failed, and were cut off; and the people crossed over opposite Jericho. Then the priests who bore the ark of the covenant of the LORD stood firm on dry ground in the midst of the Jordan; and all Israel crossed over on dry ground, until all the people had crossed completely over the Jordan. (Joshua 3:9–17)

How much faith does it take to gather an entire nation, have them pack up all their belongings, and march them headlong into a raging river? Moses could at least stand still and watch the waters of the Red Sea divide before him (Ex. 14:21). But Joshua was commanded to march directly into the river; the only indication it would miraculously subside was God's promise that it would.

Only when the priests' toes entered the swirling waters did the river's flow cease. God could have parted the river the night before or He could have stopped the waters moments before the Israelites arrived. But He chose to stretch their faith. The way God performed this miracle was a test of His people, and it certainly proved Joshua's unwavering trust in Him.

By withholding His intervention until the last possible moment, God allowed His people to demonstrate their entrenched confidence in Him. A desperate situation became a moment of triumph for God's people. They could henceforth remember this day as a time when they stepped out in faith and God was there to walk with them.

PERSONAL RESPONSE

Give an example—from your own life or the life of someone you know—of a desperate situation that became a moment of triumph:

_____

_____

_____

How did that event or experience impact your faith, or the faith of others?

_____

_____

_____

What are some of the challenges associated with trusting God to intervene in your life?

_____

_____

_____

Joshua acted on God's word even when it appeared such trust could lead to disaster. Someone who has not heard God speak as Joshua had might consider their actions merely reckless abandon caused by misguided presumption upon God. Yet when you have a promise from God, stepping out in faith is the most logical and reasonable thing you can do. It is not presumptuous to step out in obedience when you have just heard God speak.

PERSONAL RESPONSE

Recall an experience in which you, or someone you know, received God's provision at the last moment. Why do you believe God delayed His provision?

_____

_____

_____

How do you differentiate between presumption and faith when it comes to expecting God to meet your needs?

_____

_____

_____

The reason more people do not see Jordan Rivers parting in their lives and ministries is because they waver at the riverbank.

The reason more people do not see Jordan Rivers parting in their lives and ministries is because they waver at the riverbank. They want to be people of faith, but they conclude it would be much easier if God would part the waters *before* they had to get their feet wet!

Too often Christians begin to step out in obedience, but they lose their nerve. They decide if God wanted them to cross the river, He would have already parted the waters. They interpret the unchanged waters as a closed door. God must not want them to proceed or He would have given them an open door.

But God may be testing their faith. Perhaps He is watching to see what they will do with a word from Him. Only God knows how many miracles spiritual leaders have missed because they turned away from the river just before God planned to part the waters.

ADDED INSIGHT INTO SPIRITUAL LEADERSHIP

REVELATION OR VISION?

There is a significant difference between revelation and vision. Vision is something people *produce*. Revelation is something people *receive*. Leaders can dream up a vision, but they cannot dream up God's will. God must reveal His will. The secular world ignores God's will, so nonbelievers are left with one alternative—to project their own vision. Christians, however, are called to a totally different approach. For Christians, God alone sets the agenda. Our goal is to discern what it is that God is revealing to us and for us.

Have you ever been part of an organization that produced a vision statement that was man-made, rather than God-revealed? What were the results?

> **Vision is something people *produce*. Revelation is something people *receive*.**

_____

_____

_____

_____

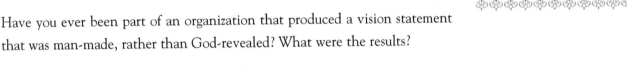

DAY THREE

FAITH FOR THE FUTURE

When you consider the enormity of the task of conquering and inhabiting Canaan, you realize how astounding God's promise to the Israelites was! He was giving them a beautiful, fertile land (Num. 34:1–12). Its expansive territory spanned from the lands east of the Jordan River all the way west to the Mediterranean Sea; from the northern region of Mount Hor to the southern wilderness of Zin. Canaan was home to numerous fortresses and fortified cities. It was a land whose current occupants would zealously resist the trespass of unwelcome intruders, yet God said the land already belonged to the Israelites!

After Joshua conquered the Canaanites, God specifically guided him in parceling out the land (Josh. 15–21). It is striking how meticulous God's instructions were. Bible scholars find the lists so detailed, several of the territories mentioned are unknown to modern historians. God is that way. He deals in specifics, not in generalities. His plan for His people was tailor-made down to the last detail. For the Israelites to settle for anything less would have been to accept less than God's specific will for them.

PERSONAL RESPONSE

What is required for a person to hear *all* the specifics about God's plan?

In some cases Joshua allotted to tribes land that had not yet even been fully conquered. Yet Joshua treated them as already taken, based on God's promise:

> So the LORD gave to Israel all the land of which He had sworn to give to their fathers, and they took possession of it and dwelt in it. The LORD gave them rest all around, according to all that He had sworn to their fathers. And not a man of all their enemies stood against them; the LORD delivered all their enemies into their hand. Not a word failed of any good thing which the LORD had spoken to the house of Israel. All came to pass. (Joshua 21:43–45)

Christians often share with us their stories of how they received a clear word from God but they allowed circumstances to sidetrack them from following through. Some have said God spoke to them as teenagers about eventually serving in international missions. But years went by and they never pursued the call. Now they are middle-aged, and they wonder if God could still use their lives in some way on the mission field.

Parents have shared with us how God told them their child would one day serve the Lord in Christian ministry. But their child was not currently walking closely with the Lord, so the parents assumed God had retracted His promise.

God promises all believers that nothing can separate them from His love. But a serious illness develops and they assume God must not care about them anymore. We've spoken to one whom God directed to start a business and use

UNIT 7—FAITH THAT BRINGS WALLS DOWN

its assets to support the Lord's work globally. Then logistical challenges and difficult labor issues captured the business leader's attention, and the vision God gave was abandoned.

When God makes a promise, it is critical to keep it before you. Live your life in the full anticipation that one day you will see God's promises come to pass. Discover what God said to your parents or grandparents and keep that before you as well (Isa. 55:10–11)!

CONCEPT REFLECTION

CONCEPT: When God makes a promise, it is critical to keep it before you. Live your life in the full anticipation that one day you will see God's promises come to pass.

How can you keep a promise of God before you at all times?

_____

_____

_____

How can you live in full anticipation that all God's promises will come to pass?

_____

_____

_____

When God makes a promise, it is critical to keep it before you. Live your life in the full anticipation that one day you will see God's promises come to pass.

ADDED INSIGHT INTO SPIRITUAL LEADERSHIP

PLANS, PROMISES, AND PICTURES

When God reveals His plans, He frequently does so in the form of a promise accompanied by vivid imagery. For example, when God revealed to Noah His plans for the earth, God made a promise—He would destroy all the peoples of the earth. He also gave Noah a clear image of how this promise would be fulfilled—a terrible flood would cover the earth (Gen. 6:17). Noah's ministry of preaching and building an ark were not driven by his vision of how he could best serve his community, nor by his imagining the best possible future for his society. His vision came from God's revelation or promise of an imminent flood that would destroy all mankind.

God revealed to Abraham that he would have a multitude of descendants who would bless all nations of the earth (Gen. 12:1–4). God then provided several images to help Abraham grasp the enormity of His promise—His descendants would be as countless as dust particles (Gen. 13:16), as numerous as the stars (Gen. 15:5), as innumerable as grains of sand on a seashore (Gen. 22:17).

When God promised to deliver the Israelites from their bondage, He referred to a land flowing with milk and honey (Ex. 3:8). When Christ promised to His followers an eternal home in heaven, He used the imagery of a groom coming for his bride (Rev. 19:7–9).

Has God revealed to you a promise of something He desires to do in or through you, or through an organization or ministry in which you have a leadership role? If so, what image has He given you related to that promise? _____

God made everything He had promised available to His people during Joshua's time. Yet, the Israelites never fully occupied the land God said He wanted to give them. Israel reached its largest size territorially under King David, yet by the following generation, under Solomon's reign, it began shrinking in size as the surrounding kingdoms seized its lands. The reality is that God's people never fully enjoyed all God had promised. God had much more in mind for His people than they ever received.

Much of the book of Joshua presents a paradox. We read that God *gave* the land to the Israelites, and then we find they still had to *take* it using military force. When Joshua first assumed his leadership role, he reminded the people of God's promise: "Remember the word which Moses the servant of the LORD commanded you, saying, 'The LORD your God is giving you rest and is giving you this land . . . But you shall pass before your brethren armed, all your mighty men of valor, and help them'" (Josh. 1:13–14).

This promise was conditional. God promised to *give* the land to the Israelites, but then He instructed them to enter in and to *fight* for it. That is like someone offering to give you a million dollars and then telling you to work the next twenty years in order to obtain it. It doesn't seem like much of a gift!

Perhaps Moses was earlier bewildered by the same paradox:

So I have come down to deliver them out of the hand of the Egyptians, and to bring them up from that land to a good and large land, to a land flowing with milk and honey, to the place of the Canaanites and the Hittites and the Amorites and the Perizzites and the Hivites and the Jebusites. (Exodus 3:8)

UNIT 7—FAITH THAT BRINGS WALLS DOWN

So far Moses had not heard anything objectionable. Then the Lord continued: "Come now, therefore, and I will send you to Pharaoh that you may bring My people, the children of Israel, out of Egypt" (Ex. 3:10).

By this point Moses is stammering, "Wait a minute, Lord. I thought *You* were going to deliver the children of Israel. Why are You sending *me?*"

God clarified His plan: He was indeed planning to free Israel, but He was going to use Moses to do it. Using people to carry out His redemptive work is a practice God uses throughout the Bible and throughout history.

PERSONAL RESPONSE

How can you balance a sure promise from God with old-fashioned effort?

_____

_____

_____

Are there risks associated with pursuing what seems to be a sure promise from God? If so, what are they? If not, why not?

_____

_____

_____

Why do you believe God would allow a person to make a sacrificial effort when His promise of a good outcome seems certain?

_____

_____

_____

Could God have simply evacuated the cities of Canaan, leaving only a welcome mat set outside the city gate? Certainly. God could have sent His death angel to exterminate every living thing in Canaan while the Israelites were still breaking camp east of the Jordan River. God could have put it into the hearts of the Canaanites to pack up their belongings and to move to Mesopotamia before the Israelites arrived. Yet God did not.

God's primary concern was not giving His people land; it was developing a relationship. On Mount Sinai, God said, "You have seen what I did to the Egyptians, and how I bore you on eagles' wings and brought you to Myself" (Ex. 19:4).

The promised land was simply the means God used to establish a unique relationship of trust and obedience with His people.

The promised land was simply the means God used to establish a unique relationship of trust and obedience with His people. Had the Israelites simply rushed into an evacuated Canaan and moved into the homes and farms, they would have quickly forgotten their Lord. That would have defeated the whole purpose for God's delivering them.

Instead, God allowed them to face one challenge after another. At every turn, they realized that without God's intervention, they would fail. Their lives depended on God's presence. The Israelites would therefore do everything possible to ensure God was pleased with them and that He would remain in their midst.

God's promises to His people are plentiful. Yet so many Christians do not experience them simply because they don't claim them. Notice some of the profound promises available to every Christian:

- So I say to you, ask, and it will be given to you; seek, and you will find; knock, and it will be opened to you. For everyone who asks receives, and he who seeks finds, and to him who knocks it will be opened. (Luke 11:9–10)

- Come to Me, all you who labor and are heavy laden, and I will give you rest. Take My yoke upon you and learn from Me, for I am gentle and lowly in heart, and you will find rest for your souls. For My yoke is easy and My burden is light. (Matthew 11:28–30)

- Therefore if the Son makes you free, you shall be free indeed. (John 8:36)

- I am the vine, you are the branches. He who abides in Me, and I in him, bears much fruit; for without Me you can do nothing. (John 15:5)

- So Jesus answered and said to them, "Have faith in God. For assuredly, I say to you, whoever says to this mountain, 'Be removed and be cast into the sea,' and does not doubt in his heart, but believes that those things he says will be done, he will have whatever he says. Therefore I say to you, whatever things you ask when you pray, believe that you receive them, and you will have them." (Mark 11:22–24)

PERSONAL RESPONSE

What does it mean to claim a promise of God?

_____

_____

_____

What is the difference between claiming a conditional promise and an unconditional promise?

_____

_____

_____

_____

These are powerful promises and each is available to every Christian. Yet believers are still reluctant to seek God. They are still soul-weary. They remain in bondage. They are still hesitant to trust God for all the resources He has promised.

No doubt the reason lies in the promises themselves. Quite often God's promises come on the condition of some action on our part. For example: "Draw near to God and He will draw near to you. Cleanse your hands, you sinners; and purify your hearts, you double-minded" (James 4:8).

This is not a blanket promise assuring God's presence regardless of our lifestyles. We are required to cleanse ourselves of our sin and *then* we will experience God's presence. We must be willing to fulfill our obligations to God and not focus exclusively on what we think God's obligation is to us.

Joshua faced this truth at the outset of his leadership. God promised: "Every place that the sole of your foot will tread upon I have given you" (Josh. 1:3). God wasn't going to give Joshua something he did not step out and claim.

The Israelites couldn't remain on the eastern shores of the Jordan River and experience God's promise in Canaan. If they wanted the land, they would have to set foot on it. Joshua learned that God does not grant us His promises by default; we have to claim them.

Our lack of faith is usually the root cause for missing God's promises. As Joshua's life drew to a close, he reminded his people of God's faithfulness: "Behold, this day I am going the way of all the earth. And you know in all your hearts and in all your souls that not one thing has failed of all the good things which the LORD your God spoke concerning you. All have come to pass for you; not one word of them has failed" (Josh. 23:14).

There was no doubt in Joshua's mind that God would always be reliable. The unknown variable was what people would do when God spoke to them. Heavy on Joshua's heart was the hope that his countrymen would stay true to God. He exhorted his nation to uphold their part of the covenant with God:

And the LORD your God will expel them from before you and drive them out of your sight. So you shall possess their land, as the LORD your God promised

**All that stood
between God's
people and God's
promises was
their obedience.**

you. Therefore be very courageous to keep and to do all that is written in the Book of the Law of Moses, lest you turn aside from it to the right hand or to the left. (Joshua 23:5–6)

All that stood between God's people and God's promises was their obedience. They could choose their fate by trusting God or by doubting Him. The same is true for every believer; God stands ready to fulfill every promise. All He needs to see is our obedience.

CONCEPT REFLECTION

CONCEPT: **All that stood between God's people and God's promises was their obedience.**

Describe the challenge a leader faces in helping other people to trust God:

_____

_____

_____

_____

_____

DAY FOUR

FAITH THAT FOSTERS COURAGE

An obvious symptom of weak faith is fear. Fear is the by-product of a lack of trust in God.

One can draw the wrong conclusion about Joshua because God often exhorted His faithful general to "be strong and of good courage" (Josh. 1:6–7, 9; 10:8; 11:6). Those of us who have never fought in combat may not understand the significance of God's words.

Joshua never demonstrated fear or cowardice. In fact, at times he revealed great courage. But God knows the human heart. No one is immune to fear, especially those in positions of great danger. The fact God spoke such words indicates God knew Joshua needed to hear them. Joshua's greatest fear would be for God to abandon him. Hence God's assurance: "As I was with Moses, so I will be with you. I will not leave you nor forsake you" (Josh. 1:5).

> ### JOSHUA 1:9
> *"Have I not commanded you? Be strong and of good courage; do not be afraid, nor be dismayed, for the LORD your God is with you wherever you go."*

What does it mean to be strong and of good courage in a difficult situation you may be facing today?

_____

_____

_____

_____

It is crucial that Christian leaders recognize God's voice. It may be the only thing standing between them and disaster.

No one could blame Joshua if he felt intimidated by his enemies. They were purportedly giants! Their cities were fiercely defended. Joshua was not unaware of the dangers of his assignment but, once God spoke, Joshua's confidence was like granite.

The reason some spiritual leaders struggle with fear is because they have not heard their Lord speak. The world is filled with evil people and terrifying situations. If not for God's powerful presence, many Christians would live in constant dread. It is crucial that Christian leaders recognize God's voice. It may be the only thing standing between them and disaster.

Fear has an immobilizing effect on Christians, especially on spiritual leaders. What do leaders fear? Failure. Being misunderstood. Humiliation. Responsibility for others' suffering. Criticism.

Leaders bear the added pressure of knowing their mistakes can cost others dearly. Leaders have innumerable occasions for fear. They, of all people, must rely on God's wisdom. Their courage must come from God and not from their own self-reliance. Following God's leading can appear precarious to those who focus on the difficult circumstances before them.

When Joshua began leading his people into Canaan, he remembered how, forty years earlier, his colleagues and the leading experts of his day pronounced the conquering of Canaan too risky and dangerous. Now Joshua was setting out to do exactly that. He was endangering not only his life but the life of every soldier who joined him. If ever he needed courage, now was the time.

PERSONAL RESPONSE

How might a person overcome feelings of intimidation in the face of a powerful or intimidating enemy?

_____

_____

_____

How might a person overcome the immobilizing effects of fear?

_____

_____

_____

Of what or whom are *you* most afraid? _____

What might you do to overcome that fear?

_____

_____

_____

ANOTHER LEADER IN GOD'S WORD

JEHOSHAPHAT: COURAGEOUS DECISION-MAKING

King Jehoshaphat was a godly king in a tumultuous time. When he received word that the armies of the Moabites, Ammonites, and Meunites were about to attack Jerusalem, Jehoshaphat knew that he lacked the military resources to repel their invasion. The commonly accepted practice would have been for him to appeal for peace and accept the terms his oppressors demanded. Such a decision, however, would likely mean the death of thousands of his subjects, as well as the end of his own rule and perhaps his own death. The king wisely turned to God for guidance.

Jehoshaphat led the people into a time of fasting and prayer. He stood among the people in the new court of the house of the Lord and cried out to God, "O our God, will You not judge them? For we have no power against this great multitude that is coming against us; nor do we know what to do, but our eyes are upon You" (2 Chron. 20:12).

God spoke to the people through the prophet Jahaziel, saying, "Do not be afraid nor dismayed because of this great multitude, for the battle is not yours, but God's. Tomorrow go down against them . . . you will find them at the end of the brook before the Wilderness of Jeruel. You will not need to fight in this battle. Position yourselves, stand still and see the salvation of the LORD" (2 Chron. 20:15–17).

Jehoshaphat took courage from God's word, and he ordered the choir to precede the army out of the city into battle. No king had ever before given such an unorthodox order to his people at the beginning of a battle. Nevertheless, the choir went forward at Jehoshaphat's command, singing, "Praise the LORD, for His mercy endures forever" (2 Chron. 20:21). And it was as they sang praises, the Lord set ambushes against the enemy troops so that when Jehoshaphat's choir members and soldiers arrived on the scene, they saw nothing but dead bodies and immense spoil—so much spoil, in fact, that it took them three days to gather up the wealth of the fallen armies.

What is God saying to you today about how you might lead your organization through a difficult time?

_____

_____

_____

DAY FIVE

FAITH THAT FINDS REST

Just as faith is the remedy for fear, trusting in God also brings a sense of emotional and spiritual rest. Rest was a dominant theme throughout Joshua's life (Josh. 1:13, 15; 11:23; 14:15; 22:4; 23:1).

Joshua spoke to the tribes of Reuben, Gad, and Manasseh about rest: "Remember the word which Moses the servant of the LORD commanded you, saying, 'The LORD your God is giving you rest and is giving you this land'" (Josh. 1:13).

Later, after the invasion was concluded, we read:

The LORD gave them rest all around, according to all that He had sworn to their fathers. And not a man of all their enemies stood against them; the LORD delivered all their enemies into their hand. Not a word failed of any good thing which the LORD had spoken to the house of Israel. All came to pass. (Joshua 21:44–45)

The concept of rest would have been especially poignant for the Israelites. Their parents had grown up in slavery where exhaustion was a matter of course. The current generation had spent forty years wandering in the wilderness. Their nomadic lifestyle took them everywhere but to the promised land. The tension must have been palpable those four long decades.

Month by month, funeral by funeral, the people gloomily waited for the demise of their unfaithful leaders. Those who had wept with fear at the edge of Canaan now suffered the stares of recrimination from those who were squandering their youth in a barren wilderness.

Then, when the Israelites finally entered Canaan, they experienced anything but rest. Invading enemy territory, they were in a foreign and hostile land. The Israelites had to remain in a state of constant battle readiness. Long marches, grueling days, sleepless nights—the Israelite warriors must have longed for rest.

PERSONAL RESPONSE

From what do you most desire to experience rest? _____
What might you do to maintain a faith-filled courage to move forward, when the desired rest seems elusive?

_____

_____

_____

Physical exhaustion was only one part of the Israelites' weariness. Emotionally, they were stretched to the breaking point. They were separated from their families. They were regularly exposed to violence. They had to kill or be killed. They lost comrades in battle. The possibility of ambush would have kept them constantly on edge.

Spiritually, they were paying a price as well for the sins of their fathers. Instead of enjoying the promised land for the last forty years as God had intended, they were just now struggling to wrest the territory from the Canaanites.

They knew they were not yet where God wanted them to be. The psalmist said, "For forty years I was grieved with that generation, and said, 'It is a people who go astray in their hearts, and they do not know My ways.' So I swore in My wrath, 'They shall not enter My rest'" (Ps. 95:10–11).

And for forty years they did not. The writer of Hebrews, referring to the tragic experience of the Israelites, apprised his own generation of the connection between faith and rest:

> And to whom did He swear that they would not enter His rest, but to those who did not obey? So we see that they could not enter in because of unbelief. Therefore, since a promise remains of entering His rest, let us fear lest any of you seem to have come short of it. For indeed the gospel was preached to us as well as to them; but the word which they heard did not profit them, not being mixed with faith in those who heard it. For we who have believed do enter that rest. (Hebrews 3:18–4:3)

A tormented soul does not experience God's rest. Guilt and anxiety wage war on the spirit, eliminating any hope of peace. Though people surround themselves with safe and comfortable circumstances, they may still lack the restful peace that only God can give. God's rest comes in the midst of all situations. Those who walk closely with God experience a sense of rest that cannot be explained in physical terms.

A tormented soul does not experience God's rest.

CONCEPT REFLECTION

CONCEPT: **A tormented soul does not experience God's rest.**

What are some things that can torment a soul?

_____

_____

_____

How can a person live free from anxiety?

_____

_____

_____

The rest God brings to the soul is so deep that nothing can disturb it. The apostle Paul aptly described God's rest as a peace that surrounds your heart and mind and cannot be shaken, regardless of your circumstances (Phil. 4:6–7).

It is a peace that comes to those who know they have faithfully carried out God's will. It is experiencing God's pleasure. It is a profound blessing only God can give. Such was the rest Joshua and his people experienced. As they trusted and obeyed God, they entered His rest.

BIBLE CONTEMPLATION

PHILIPPIANS 4:6–7

"Be anxious for nothing, but in everything by prayer and supplication, with thanksgiving, let your requests be made known to God; and the peace of God, which surpasses all understanding, will guard your hearts and minds through Christ Jesus."

What are the prerequisites for experiencing God's peace?

_____

_____

_____

Is there something you need to do today to experience more of God's peace?

_____

_____

_____

COMPLETE TRUST

Several strong traits defined Joshua, but his most prominent characteristic was his complete trust in God. His faith led him to stand firm for God, even against the jibes and threats of his own colleagues. His faith sustained him even when he could not see the end result of God's promises.

Joshua's faith was not blind faith in the sense of being based on what he did *not* know about God. His trust was firmly established by what he *did* understand to be true. Joshua's faith gave him courage to face any enemy. His courage provided compelling testimony to his faith.

Finally, Joshua's faith led him to experience an indescribable sense of God's rest. God brought peace to Joshua's life. No enemy could rob him of that. Joshua's faith brought the people of God to experience all the promises of God in a land of rest.

Joshua's faith brought the people of God to experience all the promises of God in a land of rest.

UNIT 8

INFLUENCE THAT MATTERS

> *And the children of Israel did so, just as Joshua commanded, and took up twelve stones from the midst of the Jordan, as the LORD had spoken to Joshua, according to the number of the tribes of the children of Israel, and carried them over with them to the place where they lodged, and laid them down there. Then Joshua set up twelve stones in the midst of the Jordan, in the place where the feet of the priests who bore the ark of the covenant stood; and they are there to this day . . .*
>
> *About forty thousand prepared for war crossed over before the LORD for battle, to the plains of Jericho. On that day the LORD exalted Joshua in the sight of all Israel; and they feared him, as they had feared Moses, all the days of his life.*
>
> JOSHUA 4:8–9, 13–14

A leader's words hold enormous power. A leader's statement can bind people or it can set them free. A pronouncement from a leader can unite people or it can divide them. A leader's influence can inspire people to accomplish the seemingly impossible or it can demoralize them, rendering them useless. A leader can bless people or curse them.

Joshua's credibility as a leader cannot be overstated. Only a person with tremendous influence could have mobilized a motley crew of nomads to invade a terrifying land teeming with giants and boasting powerful chariots and impregnable fortresses. Influence is a difficult thing to describe.

A leader's words hold enormous power.

DAY ONE

JOSHUA WAS DRIVEN BY GOD'S AGENDA

Secular leaders are motivated by their own objectives or the expectations of their boards of governors, their bosses, or their colleagues. Economic markets or political factors are significant forces in the secular leadership realm. Conversely, spiritual leaders are driven by *God's* agenda. God determines where people ought to be and spiritual leaders strive, under God's direction, to move their people to the place God has for them.

Spiritual leaders face two considerable challenges. The first is to clearly identify God's agenda for their people. If they do not understand God's will and if they are unfamiliar with His voice, they will be forced to generate their own vision and hope it pleases God. As we have seen, Joshua regularly communed with God and always understood the Lord's will. His success depended entirely upon this fact.

The second challenge for spiritual leaders comes at the point of influence. Once leaders know where God wants their people to be, how do they move them to get there? We have met numerous leaders who resigned their positions or were relieved of them because they were unable to move their people from where they were to where God wanted them to be.

There are pastors who have left their churches after serving only a few months because the people refused to follow them. To know where your people *ought* to be and yet to be unable to get them there is one of the most frustrating experiences leaders endure.

Joshua knew exactly what God wanted for the Israelites. They were to walk with God in holiness, and as they obeyed Him they would capture Canaan. The objective was clear; how to accomplish it was the question. Moses, the revered prophet, was unable to lead these people to fully accomplish God's will.

If the venerable Moses had failed, what hope did Joshua have? If the obstinate people chronically complained and grumbled against Moses, wouldn't Joshua expect to face the same rebellious attitudes from the next generation? Yet Joshua *was* successful. The people *did* follow him. Influence is somewhat of a mystery. Examining Joshua's life will shed some light on how leaders exert influence on followers.

ADDED INSIGHT INTO SPIRITUAL LEADERSHIP

ELEMENTS OF LEADERSHIP

Spiritual leadership has a number of elements, most notably these:

1. The challenge of moving people from where they are to where God wants them to be

2. Dependency on the Holy Spirit to produce ultimate results

To know where your people *ought* to be and yet to be unable to get them there is one of the most frustrating experiences leaders endure.

3. Accountability to God for those under their leadership

4. Influence on all people, not just God's people

5. Discerning and following through on God's agenda

Which of these statements do you personally find the most challenging? Why?

_____

_____

_____

CONCEPT REFLECTION

CONCEPT: Spiritual leaders are driven by *God's* agenda.

What factors are involved in determining God's agenda for your life?

_____

_____

_____

What factors are involved in determining God's agenda for those you lead?

_____

_____

_____

**Spiritual leaders
are driven by
God's agenda.**

What is the link between making yourself accessible to God and determining God's agenda for your life and your organization?

_____

_____

_____

JOSHUA WAS ACCESSIBLE

A leader's accessibility has been a topic of debate for generations. History's leaders have all had to choose what their relationship would be with those they led.

Joshua led his soldiers from amid their ranks. He did not have a magnificent chariot to ride in or even a powerful stallion to carry him. When he commanded his men to march through the night, he marched with them. When he ordered his men to attack superior forces, he fought with them.

We are never told that Joshua enjoyed a luxurious general's quarters or that his food or his living conditions were superior to his men's. Joshua's men enthusiastically followed him because he fought with them, endured hardships with them, and never asked them to do something he was unwilling to do himself.

PERSONAL RESPONSE

How are you accessible to the people you lead?

_____

_____

_____

Do you need to become more accessible? If so, how could you become more accessible?

_____

_____

_____

Are there factors that keep you from being as accessible as you'd like to be? If so, how could you overcome them?

_____

_____

_____

DAY TWO

JOSHUA REMAINED CONFIDENT

Confidence is a must for an effective leader. People do not follow wishy-washy leaders. Most of history's famous leaders have had confidence in themselves.

CONCEPT REFLECTION

CONCEPT: **Confidence is a must for an effective leader.**

Confidence is a must for an effective leader.

How do you project confidence to those you lead?

_____

_____

_____

Do you need to project greater confidence? If so, how could you do this?

_____

_____

_____

The confidence of great leaders does not come from their size, strength, or social status but from within themselves. Two of the hallmarks of this inner quality of confidence are an optimistic attitude and a positive demeanor, regardless of circumstances.

CONCEPT REFLECTION

CONCEPT: Great leaders intentionally maintain optimistic attitudes and a positive demeanor, regardless of their circumstances.

How do you manifest an optimistic attitude and a positive demeanor to those you lead?

_____

_____

Great leaders intentionally maintain optimistic attitudes and a positive demeanor, regardless of their circumstances.

Do you need to manifest a more optimistic attitude? A more positive demeanor? If so, what could you do?

_____

_____

_____

What difficulties do you face in _sustaining_ an optimistic attitude or a positive demeanor?

_____

_____

_____

How could you overcome these difficulties?

_____

_____

_____

_____

Joshua always spoke boldly of certain victory, but, unlike most of history's military leaders, the source of Joshua's confidence was not his own military ability. Rather, his assurance came from God. His solid faith in God's ability is obvious from his reconnaissance report of Canaan:

> The land we passed through to spy out is an exceedingly good land. If the LORD delights in us, then He will bring us into this land and give it to us, "a land which flows with milk and honey." Only do not rebel against the LORD, nor fear the people of the land, for they are our bread; their protection has departed from them, and the LORD is with us. Do not fear them. (Numbers 14:7–9)

Joshua did not have to force himself to sound confident for the sake of morale; he *was* confident. Throughout the conquest of Canaan, Joshua continually encouraged the people to remain steadfast because God was with them. Just as God's presence ensured Joshua and his soldiers of victory, it simultaneously discouraged and demoralized their enemies (Josh. 2:10–11; 9:24).

People take their cues from their leaders. When leaders grow discouraged and give up, it is totally disheartening for their followers. Leaders often carry more pressure and responsibility than their followers—all the more reason to demonstrate confidence and model a positive attitude. The Israelites took their cues from Joshua and because he was so confident in the Lord, they always entered battle correctly assuming they would win.

People take their cues from their leaders.

PERSONAL RESPONSE

Give an example of when morale among your followers improved as a result of something you did or said:

_____

_____

_____

_____

UNIT 8—INFLUENCE THAT MATTERS

Give an example of when morale among your followers declined as a result of something you did or said, or something you did not do or say:

_____

_____

_____

JOSHUA REMAINED TRUSTWORTHY

Soldiers are accustomed to obeying orders. They generally comply with reasonable instructions. They may even follow questionable commands. But some of Joshua's commands would have seemed downright ludicrous.

Picture a military commander ordering his men to march around an enemy fortress once a day for six days and then circle it seven times on the seventh day. For added measure, Joshua commanded seven priests to blow on rams' horns and the soldiers to shout (Josh. 6:8–21). Such a battle plan seemed absurd, except for the knowledge that it came from God.

Imagine a general ordering a soldier and his family to be stoned to death just for keeping some loot from a captured enemy city. It seems excessively harsh, but God had His reasons for commanding it.

Consider a commander in chief ordering his soldiers to march thirty-five kilometers throughout the night so that at sunup they could fight against five kings and their armies, all of whom had enjoyed a good night's sleep (Josh. 10:9).

Visualize a general stopping in the middle of a fierce battle and, in front of his troops and his foes, praying for the sun to stand still so they could complete their victory (Josh. 10:12–13)! These were unusual practices for a general—to say the least! Yet we hear of no complaints from Joshua's men. There was no rebellion or insubordination. They trusted that he knew what he was doing.

Why is it some leaders can call for great sacrifice and exertion and their people seem happy to comply, while other leaders cannot even make minimal requests without stubborn resistance from their subordinates? Usually it is a matter of respect.

Joshua earned his people's trust. He was consistent. He lived among them and fought alongside them. His track record proved he heard from God and that God was blessing his leadership (Josh. 4:14). Joshua's army experienced victory everywhere they went. Joshua had won the trust of his followers. When Joshua was leading, they would follow him anywhere and take on any foe.

Modern leaders sometimes misjudge the level of confidence people have in them. Merely occupying a leadership position does not make one a leader. Relying on positional influence is the most anemic way to lead. People may give you the benefit of the doubt initially, but they will be watching to see how and where you are leading them. Almost anyone can obtain a leadership position. But only men and women of integrity and sound character earn the respect that defines a true leader.

PERSONAL RESPONSE

What is involved in earning the respect of those you lead?

_____

_____

_____

ANOTHER LEADER IN GOD'S WORD

DAVID: BE CAREFUL WHAT YOU ASK

No leader should ever ask a follower to do something that the leader would be unwilling to do. Neither should a leader ever influence a follower to do something that brings glory or satisfaction only to the leader. Influence needs to be exerted in ways that bring benefit to the overall organization, benefit to the follower, and glory to God.

At one point, David was camped near Bethlehem, which was occupied by a Philistine garrison at the time. He remarked wistfully, "Oh, that someone would give me a drink of the water from the well of Bethlehem, which is by the gate!" (2 Sam. 23:15). Three of David's loyal followers immediately set out for the well, "broke through the camp of the Philistines" (2 Sam. 23:16), drew water from the well, and brought it back to David. David was appalled at what he had said and they had done. He had influenced three of his most loyal soldiers to endanger their lives. He saw the water they had brought him as far too valuable a commodity to drink—rather, he poured it out to the Lord, saying, "Far be it from me, O LORD, that I should do this! Is this not the blood of the men who went in jeopardy of their lives?" (2 Sam. 23:17).

Are you influencing—even subconsciously—those around you to do things that are only for your self-interest? _____ In what ways do you need to guard more carefully what you say, so that you might influence others to do only what brings benefit to *them*?

_____

_____

_____

In what ways do you need to guard more carefully what you say so that you always advance the overall organization?

_____

_____

_____

In what ways do you need to guard more carefully what you say so that you always bring glory to God?

_____

_____

_____

JOSHUA WORKED WELL WITH ASSOCIATES

It should come as no surprise that Joshua worked well with his associates. God had assigned him to an associate's role for forty years. Moses seemed to struggle in working with other people. He was dismal at delegation and tended to do everything himself (Ex. 18).

Moses faced rebellion from many of his key leaders. The ten "holdout" spies, chief leaders of their respective tribes, did not support him. Interestingly, when these ten men vehemently argued against invading Canaan, Moses did not speak up or interrupt. Even his closest associates, including his siblings Aaron and Miriam, criticized his leadership (Num. 12). Whether it was due to the nature of his followers or the nature of his leadership style, Moses was plagued by insubordination and complaining from all sides during his tenure as a leader.

Joshua seemed better able to deal with associates. Joshua's father-in-law never had to take him aside and teach him how to work with others. It seemed to come instinctively to Joshua. Joshua's associates did not intimidate him, though they were strong leaders themselves. We don't read of any adversarial relationships in Joshua's camp. Obviously Joshua knew how to treat associates and how to take them with him as he walked with God.

The refusal to heed advice has been the undoing of many a leader. One of

The refusal to heed advice has been the undoing of many a leader.

Joshua's strength was his willingness to receive counsel from his associates. Joshua sought the assistance of the elders in determining what to do with the Gibeonite messengers (Josh. 9:3–27). Perhaps if Joshua had sought the help of the Lord rather than the elders, he would not have been fooled (Josh. 9:14)!

Joshua also worked with the elders of the various tribes along with the high priest to equitably divide the land among the twelve tribes (Josh. 19:51). When Joshua had grown old and was preparing to retire from active leadership, he "called for all Israel, for their elders, for their heads, for their judges, and for their officers" (Josh. 23:2).

PERSONAL RESPONSE

Are you ever reluctant to accept the advice of others? If so, why?

_____

_____

_____

What criteria do you use in evaluating advice you receive?

_____

_____

_____

In an age before loudspeakers and megaphones, it would have been extremely difficult for Joshua to address an entire nation. So he called the leaders together and gave them his final charge. Joshua knew who the influential people of his nation were. He knew how to influence them. He did not alienate them by claiming the credit for their success or by hoarding the limelight. His impact on his associates was so profound that even after his death, they continued to heed what he had said (Judg. 2:7).

Good leaders identify and win over key leaders in their organizations. Carried out with the wrong motive, this can be stark manipulation. But when leaders seek to bring others on board by communicating with them and developing a relationship with them, that is good leadership.

Foolish are the leaders who neglect the influencers of their organizations. It is a mistake to assume everyone will accept a vision merely because it comes from the leader. Joshua was always careful to communicate God's instructions to his leaders, allowing them the opportunity to respond to God and not just to God's messenger.

> **It is a mistake to assume everyone will accept a vision merely because it comes from the leader.**

PERSONAL RESPONSE

How do you identify the key influencers in your organization?

_____

_____

_____

In what ways are you developing a relationship with your key influencers?

_____

_____

_____

How are you developing unique relationships with those you lead?

_____

_____

_____

ANOTHER LEADER IN GOD'S WORD

PAUL: DEVELOPING PEOPLE

The apostle Paul wrote to the Colossians about his aim in their midst: "Him we preach, warning every man and teaching every man in all wisdom, that we may present every man perfect in Christ Jesus. To this end I also labor, striving according to His working which works in me mightily" (Col. 1:28–29). Paul made it clear that his purpose was to develop people. He sought to take them from spiritual immaturity to spiritual maturity, from disobedience to obedience, from faithlessness to fruitfulness. He took great joy in seeing people blossom into the people God desired for them to become.

What would you say to _your_ organization about your goals for the personal development of each employee or volunteer?

_____

_____

_____

It can be tempting for leaders to let busy schedules or mounds of paperwork prevent them from spending time with those working under them. Yet this can be a costly oversight. Astute leaders listen carefully to feedback from associates and derive important cues about the organization.

Sagacious leaders schedule regular meeting times with their key people to ensure they are working closely together toward their organizational goals. Joshua was obviously careful to walk with the leaders of Israel, keeping them apprised of what God had said and where they were going next.

PERSONAL RESPONSE

How could you adjust your schedule to spend more time with key influencers, associates, or advisers?

_____

_____

_____

_____

ADDED INSIGHT INTO SPIRITUAL LEADERSHIP

DEVELOPING OTHERS TO LEAD

Leaders lead followers. But great leaders lead leaders. One of the tragic mistakes many leaders make is to set themselves up as being indispensable to their organizations. Some do this because they are personally insecure, some because they like the power or notoriety of being indispensable, and others simply because they get so caught up in their work that they fail to invest time developing other leaders within the organization. Failing to develop leaders, however, sets up an organization for failure down the line. No matter how great the leader in his or her time, the leader fails if the organization ultimately fails because of a lack of ongoing successful leadership.

What might you do to improve the development of leaders within your organization?

_____

_____

_____

_____

Another Leader in God's Word

Jesus: Time with His Disciples

The Gospels tell us clearly that there were times when Jesus narrowed His focus to a select few. Certainly there were times when He delivered profound teaching to the multitudes. But at other times, He took His twelve disciples aside and taught them in a way that was more intimate and deeper than what He taught to the crowds (Matt. 10; 13:10–17; Mark 7:17–23). There were still other times when Jesus met with His inner circle of disciples—Peter, James, and John—and went still deeper into spiritual matters (Luke 9:28; Matt. 26:37–38). On occasion, Jesus invested time with just one disciple (John 20:27; 21:15–19).

Why was Jesus selective in spending time with various individuals? He knew that some people were more willing to receive His teaching and to act on it than were others. By investing in those who truly desired His life-changing truth, He was preparing them for the day when they would be powerful leaders themselves.

Is there someone in your organization today with whom you perhaps should spend some one-on-one time? _____

DAY FOUR

Joshua Influenced His Family

It seems somewhat peculiar that Scripture tells us nothing of Joshua's family. We are told about Moses' parents, his siblings, his wife and children, and even his father-in-law, but we read nothing about Joshua's family. One of the great mysteries of biblical history is why so few children of great leaders followed their parents in serving the Lord. Scripture seems to provide more warnings than positive examples:

- We know Moses had sons, but they never played a prominent role in their nation's history (Ex. 4:20, 24–26).

- Two of Aaron's sons, Nadab and Abihu, were cavalier in serving God and God took their lives in judgment (Lev. 10:1–3).

- The priest Eli had two wayward sons, both of whom died as a result of their sin (1 Sam. 2:12–17; 3:13).

- Samuel's sons were also wicked and could not live up to their father's impeccable reputation (1 Sam. 8:1–5).

We are not told if Moses' or Joshua's sons became evil or turned from following the Lord. However, it is clear that despite growing up with fathers who were mighty men of God, they did not follow in their steps as prominent leaders themselves.

While there is silence from Scripture about what Joshua's sons did, it is clear what Joshua intended for his family: "And if it seems evil to you to serve the LORD, choose for yourselves this day whom you will serve . . . But as for me and my house, we will serve the LORD" (Josh. 24:15).

Considering Joshua was a man of his word and a man of prayer, and knowing how respected he was, we may assume God blessed his desire for his family.

PERSONAL RESPONSE

In what ways do you believe you are a successful leader in your family?

_____

_____

_____

How could you be a more successful leader in your family?

_____

_____

_____

ANOTHER LEADER IN GOD'S WORD

SAMUEL: NO SUCCESSOR

As great as Samuel was as a leader of Israel, he did not prepare a successor. The Bible tells us: "Now it came to pass when Samuel was old that he made his sons judges over Israel. The name of the firstborn was Joel, and the name of his second, Abijah; they were judges in Beersheba. But his sons did not walk in his ways; they turned aside after dishonest gain, took bribes, and perverted justice" (1 Sam. 8:1–3). Because of their behavior, the elders of Israel insisted that Samuel appoint a king over them. Samuel became the last of the "judges," and as we know from the life of Saul, the king Samuel was led to anoint, Israel suffered under the rule of *most* of its kings. Sadly, Samuel failed not only as a leader in Israel, but as a *parent*.

Are you preparing someone to take over the organization you presently lead? If so, what added responsibilities do you have to train up your successors as good leaders?

_____

_____

_____

JOSHUA HAD INFLUENCE WITH GOD

It is one thing to have prestige with people; it is quite another to have influence with God. Without question, Joshua exerted a tremendous influence on people, but he also had a rich relationship with God. He was obviously extremely close to the Lord, because he regularly and confidently asked for miracles and he routinely received them.

When five Amorite kings united to attack the city of Gibeon, Joshua quickly advanced his army to join the battle. Here was an opportunity for the Israelites to defeat the king of Jerusalem and his allies in one engagement. The fighting was fierce, but God intervened against the Amorites and sent down large hailstones, killing many of them (Josh. 10:11).

The day was beginning to wane and yet the victory was not yet complete. If the enemy were allowed to regroup, they could attack the Israelites at a vulnerable moment in the future. In a most unusual prayer, Joshua asked God to hold the sun still until the battle was complete. Scripture tells us the rest of the story: "And there has been no day like that, before it or after it, that the LORD heeded the voice of a man; for the LORD fought for Israel" (Josh. 10:14).

Herein lies the difference between a secular leader and a spiritual leader. Many of their skills overlap. Both must communicate a sense of vision and direction to their followers. Both must inspire their followers and delegate work to them. Both must lead with confidence.

But only spiritual leaders can draw on God's divine resources for their work. Whether leading secular companies or Christian organizations, spiritual leaders can do so with heaven's resources at their disposal.

PERSONAL RESPONSE

What divine resources are available to you as the leader of your organization?

_____

_____

It is one thing to have prestige with people; it is quite another to have influence with God.

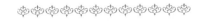

Whether leading secular companies or Christian organizations, spiritual leaders can do so with heaven's resources at their disposal.

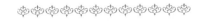

The Bible identifies certain people who enjoyed an especially intimate walk with God. During the prophet Jeremiah's ministry, God made a revealing statement: "Then the LORD said to me, 'Even if Moses and Samuel stood before Me, My mind would not be favorable toward this people'" (Jer. 15:1). What an awesome recognition to be viewed by God as one of the great prayer warriors of all time!

Abraham was another such intercessor with God and as a result, God called him His friend (James 2:23). It is one thing for us to take God seriously. It is quite another for God to respond in earnest to us!

Spiritual leaders can exert no greater influence on others than to lead with God's mighty hand upon them. When God chooses to bless leaders' efforts, nothing can stop them. Yet the time people need God most is often when they neglect Him. Hectic schedules and demanding responsibilities drive a wedge between a leader and God.

No spiritual leader is exempt from the need to maintain a close relationship with the Lord. Ironically, the busier the leader, the more time should be spent in God's presence.

Spiritual leaders can exert no greater influence on others than to lead with God's mighty hand upon them.

PERSONAL RESPONSE

What kind of intercessor with God are you?

_____

_____

_____

JOSHUA INFLUENCED THE FUTURE

The mark of extraordinary leaders is that their influence outlives them. What they do today determines what happens in the future. Although some people struggle to make a difference in their day, Joshua impacted those living centuries later. Truly this is influence on a grand scale.

When Jericho was destroyed, Joshua pronounced a curse on whoever rebuilt the city (Josh. 6:26). The ruins of Jericho symbolized God's judgment on the pagan Canaanites. God had not allowed any survivors from the city except Rahab and her family. Anyone who rebuilt the city would forfeit his sons as a consequence.

Sure enough, many years later, in the days of King Ahab, a man named Hiel laid the foundation of Jericho and rebuilt its walls. As he laid the foundation he lost his firstborn son, Abiram. As he hung the doors in the city gates his youngest son, Segub, died (1 Kings 16:34). Centuries after Joshua's day, God was still honoring the word He had spoken through Joshua.

The mark of extraordinary leaders is that their influence outlives them.

UNIT 8—INFLUENCE THAT MATTERS

PERSONAL RESPONSE

Is leaving a mark on history something a person should be concerned about? Why, or why not?

_____

_____

_____

How do you deal with the desire to leave your mark on the people or organization you lead?

_____

_____

_____

Some people attempt to influence history by their verbosity. They feel compelled to speak to every issue and to reveal everything they know. They assume if they say enough, something they utter will take root and live on in the future. Great leaders do not necessarily talk much, but what they do say is relevant and memorable.

CONCEPT REFLECTION

CONCEPT: Great leaders do not necessarily talk much, but what they do say is relevant and memorable.

How do you determine the key points you need to address in any given situation?

_____

_____

_____

How could you become more effective in addressing the great points and allowing the little ones to follow?

_____

_____

_____

Some leaders blaze into an organization in a fury of dynamic activity but then, like a fading meteorite, their influence is spent and things return to normality.

> **Great leaders do not necessarily talk much, but what they do say is relevant and memorable.**

Such people grasp everyone's attention briefly but later they are forgotten. Others not only impact the people of their generation, but their lives and words leave an ongoing legacy.

Leaders are usually people with strong opinions and a willingness to express them. But for spiritual leaders, only the words they speak that come from God will have an eternal impact. All the rest will be merely chaff. Joshua spoke for God. God's words were fulfilled and Joshua's life is remembered.

DAY FIVE

JOSHUA MOVED PEOPLE TOWARD GOD

Joshua used his influence to promote God's vision, not his own.

Most leaders have a vision for what they would like to see happen among the people they lead. But Joshua used his influence to promote *God's* vision, not his own. As a general in charge of the logistics of an army and concerned with preparing for battle, Joshua would have faced numerous legitimate and pressing concerns. Yet clearly Joshua's first priority was his people's walk with God. He placed this even above his focus on winning the next battle.

On the eve of crossing the Jordan River and entering Canaan, you might think Joshua would spend every available moment drilling his troops and having them practice with their swords and bows. Instead he declared: "Sanctify yourselves, for tomorrow the LORD will do wonders among you" (Josh. 3:5). Joshua was more concerned about his people's holiness than he was about their battle-readiness. Their holiness *was* their battle-readiness!

Joshua was more concerned about his people's holiness than he was about their battle-readiness. Their holiness *was* their battle-readiness!

CONCEPT REFLECTION

CONCEPT: Joshua was more concerned about his people's holiness than he was about their battle-readiness. Their holiness *was* their battle-readiness!

Identify one or more battles you are facing in your organization:

_____

_____

_____

_____

Define *holiness* as it relates to your organization:

_____

_____

_____

In what practical ways could holiness be manifested?

_____

_____

_____

What links do you see between your people's holiness and their battle-readiness?

_____

_____

_____

How could you influence an increase in their holiness to increase their battle-readiness?

_____

_____

_____

_____

After the Israelites had crossed the Jordan River, you might expect Joshua to act like a wary invader, anticipating a sudden attack by the defending citizens. Instead, he stopped to build a stone monument as a landmark and reminder of what God had done for them at that place (Josh. 4). Then, before going any further with the invasion, Joshua had all the males circumcised as God had commanded (Josh. 5:2–9). It is notable that in the midst of a perilous invasion, Joshua should take precious time to meticulously follow God's instructions.

Then Joshua had the people camp at Gilgal, within Canaan, so they could observe the Passover (Josh. 5:10–12). Here they were in the midst of a dangerous invasion; surely they might have put off such religious remembrances until a more opportune time. Yet Joshua made sure they stopped to worship God and to remember all He had done. Obviously he trusted God to protect them. His actions speak volumes about his priorities.

His actions speak volumes about his priorities.

Concept Reflection

CONCEPT: **Actions speak volumes about priorities.**

What do your actions tell your followers about your priorities?

_____

_____

_____

After all the religious observances had been kept, the Israelites did conquer the citizens of Jericho and Ai. But then came another unusual event. After having alerted the Canaanites to their aggressive intentions by destroying two of their cities, you would think Israel would be vigilant in preparation for a counter-assault by the hostile allied forces.

But Joshua again stopped to build an altar on Mount Ebal. There he gathered the people, and "there was not one word of all that Moses had commanded which Joshua did not read before all the assembly of Israel, with the women, the little ones, and the strangers who were living among them" (Josh. 8:35). How unusual! Instead of bracing for a counterattack, they held a worship service along with their women and children!

Obviously Joshua had a different set of priorities from the average general's. Joshua ended his term of leadership by urging a gathering of leading citizens to "hold fast to the LORD" (Josh. 23:8). During his entire time as Israel's leader, Joshua's focus was first and foremost spiritual in nature. He was a _spiritual_ leader holding the post of a military general.

Throughout Joshua's leadership he was driven by more than the desire to win battles and to be a good administrator. Joshua understood that though he was a layman, not a priest or a prophet, he was still accountable for the spiritual well-being of those placed under his care. He knew that one day he would give an account to the eternal Judge, not for the success of his military maneuvers, but for the spiritual condition of his followers. So, he was diligent to see that they walked closely with God.

Personal Response

How are you accountable for the spiritual well-being of those placed under your leadership?

_____

_____

_____

_____

How is this accountability the same for both secular organizations and spiritual organizations?_____

ADDED INSIGHT INTO
SPIRITUAL LEADERSHIP

BRINGING GLORY TO GOD

Whether people lead Christian or secular organizations, their goal ought to be to bring glory to God. Too many organizations, however—including churches, Christian schools, and Christian charities—seem more concerned about building their own reputation and elevating the profile of their organization than about bringing glory to God. It is the leader's responsibility to establish this focus and maintain it.

How do people bring glory to God? By revealing God's nature to a watching world. Even a secular business can bring God glory if the leader reflects the character of Christ; if the tenor of the business environment is one of forgiveness, patience, service, honesty, and integrity; and if customers and vendors alike feel valued and respected.

In what ways does your organization bring glory to God?

_____

_____

_____

How might you begin to change the way you do business or conduct ministry to bring God greater glory?

_____

_____

_____

A LASTING IMPACT

Joshua was unable to conquer every portion of the land of Canaan while he led his people, but Joshua was undoubtedly a person of great influence. Nothing stayed the same after Joshua got involved!

God was pleased to honor Joshua because Joshua was eager to honor Him.

Joshua was also a man others took seriously. His enemies certainly feared him. His people followed him. God answered his prayers. God even honored him and his words for the future. When Joshua assumed his leadership role, he oversaw a group of nomads in the desert. When he was finished, he led a nation occupying numerous cities throughout the beautiful land of Canaan.

Everything he did seemed to leave a lasting impact. No doubt that is because he stayed on God's agenda throughout his life. God was pleased to honor Joshua because Joshua was eager to honor Him. A life that makes a lasting difference for the kingdom of God—now that's influence!

JOSHUA'S LEADERSHIP PRINCIPLES

> *So Joshua made a covenant with the people that day, and made for them a statute and an ordinance in Shechem.*
>
> *Then Joshua wrote these words in the Book of the Law of God. And he took a large stone, and set it up there under the oak that was by the sanctuary of the LORD. And Joshua said to all the people, "Behold, this stone shall be a witness to us, for it has heard all the words of the Lord which He spoke to us. It shall therefore be a witness to you, lest you deny your God." So Joshua let the people depart, each to his own inheritance . . .*
>
> *Israel served the LORD all the days of Joshua, and all the days of the elders who outlived Joshua, who had known all the works of the LORD which He had done for Israel.*
>
> JOSHUA 24:25–28, 31

There is no doubt God was the reason for Joshua's magnificent success. Without divine guidance and intervention, Joshua and his ragtag band of ill-equipped soldiers would have been dashed to pieces at the hands of the Canaanites. Joshua never took credit for his military success, and we would be remiss in granting it to him now. But God did develop Joshua into an outstanding leader. Joshua practiced many of the leadership skills that are highly praised in military and corporate circles today.

DAY ONE

IMPROVING YOUR LEADERSHIP ABILITIES

At times Christian leaders tend to "spiritualize" God's work by saying, "It is all God and nothing to do with me!" It is true that everything they do of eternal significance has been inspired, empowered, and enabled by God, but this attitude can simply be an anemic excuse for poor leadership. Pastors and Christian business leaders can excuse a halfhearted effort for their organization by "waiting on God to do what only He can do."

Some Christian leaders never strive to improve their leadership skills, lest it appear they are relying too heavily on their own strength. Such an attitude ignores God's command to do *everything* as though we are doing it for Him (Col. 3:23).

God is sovereign. He can and will work through any person He chooses. Yet those who assume God will use them for His service regardless of their skills, education, or effort may be as disappointed as the indolent student who didn't bother to study for her exam and instead, "trusted in the Lord!" Leaders shortchange themselves and their followers when they grow complacent and neglect to improve their leadership abilities.

CONCEPT REFLECTION

CONCEPT: Leaders shortchange themselves and their followers when they grow complacent and neglect to improve their leadership abilities.

As you reflect back over your life, in what ways have you failed to steadily improve your leadership abilities?

_____

_____

_____

We have known pastors who loved God and loved their congregations, but were poor leaders. They were disorganized, wasted time, did not plan ahead, and they were careless in keeping appointments. They were weak at delegation; their sermons were disjointed and poorly delivered. Not surprisingly, their congregations were small and spiritually undernourished.

Often their people stoically suffered through mismanaged church programming because they loved their pastor, but they needed him to be so much more. Please hear us: not all small churches are the result of poor leadership, but today's generation is desperate for spiritual leadership, and people will go where they find it. Using the same principle, being a Christian businessman does not guarantee God's blessing on your business if you overlook solid business practices. Leadership skills are important in the kingdom of God!

Joshua's life was a good combination of wise leadership and God's blessing.

Leaders shortchange themselves and their followers when they grow complacent and neglect to improve their leadership abilities.

UNIT 9—JOSHUA'S LEADERSHIP PRINCIPLES

Joshua obviously enjoyed God's favor, but he also allowed God to work on his character. God did not choose to work through Joshua "just as he was." Rather, He chose to work *in* Joshua as He worked *through* him.

God took an uneducated, inexperienced slave from Egypt and walked with him through the years. As a result, Joshua emerged as an extremely effective spiritual leader. Joshua's life demonstrated tremendous leadership skills. We could greatly benefit from studying the work God did in Joshua.

JOSHUA GREW DURING TRANSITIONS

Life is in constant flux—the pace slackens, then quickens. Successful leaders master times of transition. History's military heroes were not constantly at war. They also had to deal with peacetime (though some spent as little time at this as possible!).

Joshua spent a great deal of his life in transition. He was a slave until Moses arrived in Egypt to deliver the Israelites from Egyptian bondage. Then he spent the next forty years preparing for the next phase of God's plan. During that time, only two adults made the transition into the promised land. Everyone else perished. How did Joshua (and Caleb) survive the dramatic changes taking place when everyone else was losing heart and dying? Joshua did two things.

1. Joshua Kept His Eyes on God

Joshua kept his eyes on God, regardless of the shifting circumstances around him. He knew that although the heavens and earth might change, God would remain constant (Mal. 3:6). Times change. Governments change. Trends and economies change. People change. Placing one's hope and trust in any of these things is foolish.

Joshua knew better; he understood God's sovereignty over his life while he dwelt in Egypt. God was Lord of his life in the wilderness, and He would still reign over the universe when Joshua entered Canaan. That would never change.

2. Joshua Made the Most of Growth Opportunities

Joshua made the most of his growth opportunities. He did not sit and stagnate, waiting for something big to happen. Even during the long transition period in the wilderness, he followed God diligently and nurtured God's presence in his life (Num. 27:18). Times of tranquil solitude, rare as they are, provide tremendous opportunities to grow closer to God. During Israel's wanderings, others were simply putting in time. But Joshua was growing, and when the transition time ended, he was the most prepared person in the entire nation to serve as leader.

PERSONAL RESPONSE

What growth opportunities are you pursuing right now?

_____

_____

_____

Transition times should never be squandered. On the contrary, God may use such times to bring about tremendous growth. Take advantage of unexpected forced downtime. If an injury pulls you out of your workplace, as you recuperate seize the opportunity to read books that will develop your skills and knowledge. If your church is between pastors, there are still numerous ways to reach out and minister to the community during the interim period. Wise leaders maximize transition periods by continually growing and seeking the Lord, so they are fully prepared for what comes next.

JOSHUA BUILT ON THE PAST

Throughout history, people in leadership positions have often been more concerned with protecting what already existed than pursuing something new. While there may have been times in history when successful leaders could be slow to embrace progress, in today's rapidly changing environment, a leader resistant to change is an albatross rather than an asset. It is also true that good leaders don't try to reinvent the wheel.

Much of today's leadership literature implies that the mark of a good leader is an automatic dissatisfaction with the status quo. A commonly held maxim is that leaders constantly seek change and relish transforming their organizations. Many pastors cite Isaiah 43:18–19: "Do not remember the former things, nor consider the things of old. Behold, I will do a new thing."

This type of leader believes that upon arriving at his new organization, he must radically transform everything. The problem with this mind-set is that the result is a waste of the enormous accumulated efforts made in the past. Rejecting an organization's history can reflect a callous disregard for what God has already accomplished.

Organizations often mistakenly assume when replacing a leader that they must enlist someone completely opposite to his or her predecessor. If the former CEO was a "people person," the next one must be a "systems person." If the previous pastor was keen on discipleship, the next pastor must be passionate about evangelism. Although there is sometimes a need to shore up deficiencies in current or former leaders, it can be a devastating mistake to reinvent your organization every time you obtain a new leader.

> Wise leaders maximize transition periods by continually growing and seeking the Lord, so they are fully prepared for what comes next.

PERSONAL RESPONSE

Identify a particular situation in your organization that appears to be calling for change:

_____

_____

_____

How are you resisting change? Why?

_____

_____

_____

Name a particular goal you have for your organization:

_____

_____

_____

In what areas would you be wise not to implement change too quickly? Why?

_____

_____

_____

Any organization under God's guidance will be following a plan God has initiated. He may add people with new skills to strengthen His work, but He is unlikely to keep changing the plan.

We are not suggesting that organizations should never change or that each succeeding leader should be a clone of his predecessor. Obviously each new leader brings unique talents and skills, and this is crucial. Organizations need to grow and mature and that calls for different styles of leadership. But over time, organizations take on values that become deeply ingrained in their fabric. Those values are ignored at the leader's peril!

Today's organizations must address their weaknesses while honoring the strengths and values they have gained over the years. New leaders must be cautious, lest they trample on the values God has instilled in an organization. The most successful leaders of tomorrow will be those who master today's transitions.

Today's organizations must address their weaknesses while honoring the strengths and values they have gained over the years.

CONCEPT REFLECTION

CONCEPT: Today's organizations must address their weaknesses while honoring the strengths and values they have gained over the years.

What weaknesses need to be addressed in the organization you lead?

_____

_____

_____

What strengths and values need to be honored in the organization you lead?

_____

_____

_____

How can weaknesses be addressed while honoring strengths?

_____

_____

_____

Joshua did not charge in with a whole new agenda for Israel. He remained true to God's original plan for His people. Scripture repeatedly says Joshua "left nothing undone of all that the LORD had commanded Moses" (Josh. 11:15). "There was not a word of all that Moses had commanded which Joshua did not read before all the assembly of Israel" (Josh. 8:35).

Joshua knew God had spoken to Moses; he had witnessed it personally! He understood his role to be a part of God's ultimate plan. Joshua was not _the_ plan. Understanding this truth would help so many people to find God's will. People should not ask: "What is God's will for my life?" but "What is God's will, and how should I adjust my life to it?"

This was Joshua's mind-set. When Joshua finally conquered Canaan and divided the land among the tribes, he clearly understood this to be a fulfillment of God's word to his ancestors many years earlier. Joshua was a much different leader than Moses had been. Joshua accomplished things Moses never did. He led the people to places Moses was unable to take them. There was much that was new under Joshua's leadership. However, Joshua applied his unique, God-given skills to the plan God had initiated long before he was born.

Great leaders don't disparage what has been handed to them by previous generations; they build on it.

PERSONAL RESPONSE

What is God's will (in general terms)?

_____

_____

_____

How could you adjust your life to God's will?

_____

_____

_____

DAY TWO

JOSHUA WAS A TEACHER

Good leaders are also good teachers. Part of Joshua's influence came from the way he instructed his people. He never assumed they would automatically know what to do or why they should do it. As soon as Joshua was installed as Israel's new leader, he began reminding his people what God had been saying to them (Josh. 1:13).

After they conquered the city of Ai, Joshua gathered the people on Mount Gerizim and Mount Ebal. Then Joshua personally read all of God's law to the people (Josh. 8:34). "There was not a word of all that Moses had commanded which Joshua did not read before all the assembly of Israel, with the women, the little ones, and the strangers who were living among them" (Josh. 8:35).

The practice of continually reminding the people of God's promises and commandments characterized Joshua's entire ministry. Even at the end of his life Joshua meticulously exhorted the people to obey God (Josh. 23:1–24:28).

CONCEPT REFLECTION

Good leaders are also good teachers.

CONCEPT: Good leaders are also good teachers.

What are you seeking to teach your followers?

_____

_____

_____

How do you measure the success of your teaching?

_____

_____

_____

How could you improve your teaching skills?

_____

_____

_____

The apostle Paul made the ability to teach a requirement for anyone serving as an overseer in the church (1 Tim. 3:2). Leaders who are too busy or impatient with their people tend to bark out commands and become agitated when performance levels don't meet their standards. Often these leaders end up doing the job themselves—to make certain it is done right. They neglect all kinds of opportunities to teach the skills they find lacking.

It is not enough to suggest a seminar or a relevant book. Some skills are best learned on the job. Often the best teacher on the job site is the person in charge. An investment of time in teaching someone today can pay huge dividends tomorrow.

CONCEPT REFLECTION

CONCEPT: An investment of time in teaching someone today can pay huge dividends tomorrow.

How have you witnessed the truth of this principle in your own life?

_____

_____

_____

> **An investment of time in teaching someone today can pay huge dividends tomorrow.**

UNIT 9—JOSHUA'S LEADERSHIP PRINCIPLES

In the lives of your children?

_____

_____

_____

In the lives of your followers in your organization?

_____

_____

_____

Some leaders refuse to invest in training their staffs for fear people will become overqualified for their jobs, demand more money, or be snatched up by the competition. However, true spiritual leaders understand their stewardship of each life God places under their influence. Spiritual leaders have a mandate to help their people become all God intends for them to be (Ezek. 34:1–10).

Inevitably other organizations will recognize quality employees and seek to hire them. However, if no other organization is impressed with your staff enough to want to hire them, that may be an indictment on either your hiring or your training practices! It ought to be a matter of great satisfaction for you to lead men and women who are highly coveted by other organizations. One of the greatest rewards of your personal leadership career may be that you help develop some of the top leaders in your field, who influence organizations all over the country and around the world.

We know college and seminary presidents who regularly see their vice presidents called as president to other schools. Some of our pastor friends can count dozens of former associates who now serve as senior pastors elsewhere. In the big scheme of things—God's kingdom—this is influence at its best. God's work is not about competition—it's about cooperation for the sake of a higher calling.

CONCEPT REFLECTION

CONCEPT: Spiritual leaders have a mandate to help their people become all God intends for them to be.

In one or two sentences, state what you believe to be your mandate as a spiritual leader:

_____

_____

Spiritual leaders have a mandate to help their people become all God intends for them to be.

_____

_____

In what ways are you seeking to build up leaders for the greater good of God's kingdom?

_____

_____

_____

JOSHUA USED LEADERSHIP TOOLS

Stories and symbols have enormous value as leadership tools. A well-told story can communicate far more than a two-hundred-page policy manual. Stories capture people's imaginations. People remember stories years after hearing them, though they may not remember the instructions they were given five minutes earlier. Stories are symbols. They can represent what is valuable to an organization. Good leaders learn how to incorporate stories into their leadership style.

Joshua regularly told the tale of how God rescued the people of Israel from Egypt and how He brought them into the promised land. Some of the veteran soldiers must have grinned and nodded their heads knowingly as their revered general began telling the familiar epic once again.

Some of his longtime followers could probably recite portions of the tale with their leader. There may have been certain points in the narrative—for example, when the ten spies frightened the people from trusting God—that the old soldiers grew emotional as Joshua recalled those painful moments.

The story was important, because it explained to everyone how the people had come to be where they were. There are various ways Joshua could have explained how God had walked with them, but Joshua wasn't a trained orator, a writer, or even a priest. He didn't present the data of their lengthy pilgrimage on a flip chart or from a dusty book. He was a layman who walked with God, so he simply chose to tell the story.

The use of other symbols is also important. A symbol is a powerful tool in the hands of a seasoned leader, whether it is a story, an actual physical monument, or a symbolic action. Joshua was a master at using symbolism to drive home truths to his followers.

When the Israelites miraculously crossed the Jordan River into Canaan, Joshua instructed a man from each tribe to collect a stone from the riverbed. Those stones were carried on the men's shoulders until they reached Gilgal, where Joshua built a monument. Joshua said:

> **A symbol is a powerful tool in the hands of a seasoned leader.**

This may be a sign among you when your children ask in time to come, saying, "What do these stones mean to you?" Then you shall answer them that the waters of the Jordan were cut off before the ark of the covenant of the LORD; when it crossed over the Jordan, the waters of the Jordan were cut off. And these stones shall be for a memorial to the children of Israel forever. (Joshua 4:6–7)

Though they had just experienced a stupendous miracle, Joshua knew the following generations would not appreciate what had happened unless it was explained to them. Whenever young Israelites came upon the crude monument, it was an opportunity for their parents to retell their awesome experience of crossing the Jordan River. Many generations later, that weathered stone monument would still stand as a testimony to God's miraculous work.

PERSONAL RESPONSE

Do you regularly tell stories or use symbols to teach and inspire your followers? Give an example:

_____

_____

_____

_____

_____

At the close of his leadership term, Joshua again used a stone as a symbol. He gathered the people and exhorted them to serve the Lord and to "put away the foreign gods which are among you, and incline your heart to the LORD God of Israel" (Josh. 24:23). Then he made a solemn covenant with the people as they swore their allegiance to God.

Once they had fully committed themselves to following God, Joshua set up a large rock under an oak tree near the tabernacle. He called the stone a silent witness to the commitment they had solemnly made with God. Every time they saw the stone in the future it would be a reminder of their sacred vow (Josh. 24:27).

In a different tone, Joshua decreed that the city of Jericho was never to be rebuilt (Josh. 6:26). The once formidable city was to lie in perpetual ruin as a stark reminder of God's judgment. No one could pass by that once mighty city without the chilling recollection of God's awesome power.

After Joshua's time, when the children of Israel ignored Joshua's plea and turned away from God, God allowed their enemies to torment and defeat them. Even as the Israelites were fleeing in fear from their enemies, the ruins of Jericho stood as a somber testimony of what God could do for His people when they walked faithfully with Him.

Likewise, when the Israelites executed the king of Ai as well as the king of Jerusalem and his four royal allies, Joshua commanded that a large mound of stones cover their graves (Josh. 8:29; 10:27). These mounds gave silent testimony to the perils of waging war against God and His people. After Israel's conquest of Canaan, the promised land was littered with graphic reminders of God's judgment on His foes.

Joshua also used symbolic actions to great effect. During the early stages of the Israelite invasion, Jerusalem's king gathered four fellow kings and united their armies to resist Joshua's forces. This was a powerful army led by five monarchs, yet with God's intervention Joshua's forces defeated them.

In the aftermath of the enemy rout, the five kings hid in a cave at Makkedah until the Israelites discovered them (Josh. 10:16). After the battle, Joshua presented the five kings to his people. The Israelites had once been terrified of these men and their armies, and that fear had cost them forty years in the wilderness.

To emphasize that there was no reason to fear God's enemies, Joshua had the five kings lie on the ground. Then Joshua had the captains of his army put their feet on the kings' necks, graphically symbolizing the total submission of these rulers to the Israelites (Josh. 10:24). It was humiliating for these once proud sovereigns, but it was an unbelievable triumph for Joshua's forces.

Clearly *no one* and *nothing* could withstand them when God was fighting for them. Joshua then killed the kings and hung their bodies from trees until evening so the entire army could witness the total subjugation of their once proud enemies. Although the military practices of that day seem barbaric to us today, the enormous positive effect of such symbolism is obvious.

The young Israelite soldiers had grown up in abject fear of these kings. They had spent year after year squandering their youth in a barren desert while their aging parents feebly justified their disobedience to God by explaining that Canaan was populated with fierce, undefeatable giants. But now they had seen these giants up close. Even their kings were ordinary men who could be humbled by God. Joshua wanted to remove any question from his soldiers' minds that when they walked obediently with God they were invincible. Throughout the remainder of Joshua's leadership, there is no mention of his soldiers ever fearing their enemies.

Leaders become masters of communication by capturing such symbolic moments.

PERSONAL RESPONSE

Describe a situation in which you or someone you know used a symbolic action:

_____

_____

_____

What were the results?

_____

_____

_____

How could you engage in a symbolic act to underscore a specific belief or implement a specific ideal?

_____

_____

_____

ADDED INSIGHT INTO
SPIRITUAL LEADERSHIP

BEARING WITNESS TO THE REVELATION

Spiritual leaders cannot prove that God has spoken to them. They can only bear witness to what God said. The key to spiritual leadership is bringing followers into a face-to-face encounter with God so they hear from God directly, not indirectly through their leader. Spiritual leaders may never convince their people they have heard from God personally, but once their people hear from God themselves, there will be no stopping them from participating in the work God is doing. That is because the Holy Spirit will take the truth, as shared by the leader, and confirm it in the hearts of the people. The leader cannot convince people that a particular direction is from God. This is the Holy Spirit's task.

How might a spiritual leader help his or her followers to receive God's revelation for themselves?

Two ways that spiritual leaders have used to help their followers receive God's revelation are:

1. The use of symbols that reflect the values and relationship God desires to have with His people
2. The use of stories that give examples of how God has worked or is working in the hearts of His people

How might you use symbols or stories to help your followers receive what you perceive to be God's revelation to you about what He desires to do in your organization or ministry?

_____

_____

_____

DAY THREE

JOSHUA REMAINED FOCUSED

From the moment Joshua took the reins of leadership, no one had any question about his intentions. Joshua clearly understood God's assignment: prepare God's people to conquer the land of Canaan and then occupy it as a holy nation for God's glory. The Israelite general never lost sight of the goal God set before him. There were no distractions. There were no delays. There were no excuses. Regardless of how formidable the enemy appeared, Joshua relentlessly moved forward to accomplish his goal. Joshua led his people onward with dogged persistence.

PERSONAL RESPONSE

How do you keep before yourself and your followers the supreme purpose or goal of your organization?

_____

_____

_____

Effective leaders know the purpose of their organization, and they focus on pursuing it. Leaders can be easily distracted by secondary matters and inadvertently neglect to accomplish their primary task. It can be tempting to concentrate so intently on the means to the end that you forget what the end is.

Preparing to attain a goal or declaring one's intent to reach a goal is not the same thing as achieving it. Some leaders focus so much attention on building teamwork in their organization that they indeed end up with a team, but it's a team that fails to accomplish its mission.

Some concentrate on problem solving to the extent that they lose sight of their goal. Some are good at planning; others are good at doing. We are not advocating a single-minded approach that excludes the important matters of team building and problem solving. However, effective leaders know that many important activities will engage their attention, but all are secondary to the primary objective of accomplishing the organization's purpose.

We know many well-meaning CEOs and pastors who have been fired. In some cases those dismissing them were their friends. The fundamental issue was not how hard they worked or whether they had integrity. The problem was that they were not getting the job done. There are many things to admire about Joshua and his leadership style, but one thing stands out: he stayed focused on his God-given mission.

CONCEPT REFLECTION

CONCEPT: Leaders can be easily distracted by secondary matters and inadvertently neglect to accomplish their primary task.

In what ways might you guard against doing this?

_____

_____

_____

Leaders can be easily distracted by secondary matters and inadvertently neglect to accomplish their primary task.

ADDED INSIGHT INTO SPIRITUAL LEADERSHIP

THE KEY QUESTION

The key question any leader must continually ask is this: Where should this organization be going? Many leaders become so focused on the day-to-day operations of their organization that they lose sight of their destination. It's not that they have no goals or aspirations—many even have detailed plans about what they hope to achieve and how they intend to pursue their goals. The problem is that they fail to examine the day-to-day decisions they make *in light of* the destination they believe is right for themselves personally or their organization. They get caught up in the means to the end.

Reflect for a moment on whether you evaluate every major decision you make in light of your ultimate goals as a leader. If not, what do you believe keeps you from maintaining sight of the long-range goal?

_____

_____

_____

How might you adjust your own decision-making process to take into consideration the key question: Where should this organization be going?

_____

_____

_____

JOSHUA HAD PASSION

Joshua was a passionate leader. He believed deeply in what God had called him to do. Today we frequently use dichotomies to categorize people: "He's a feeler" or "She's a thinker"; "He's task oriented" or "She's people oriented." Great leaders have emerged from each of these categories. From what we know of Joshua, he may well have been a "feeler." He certainly cared deeply about fulfilling God's assignment. The apostle Peter was a feeler; the apostle Paul was a thinker. Both were extremely passionate men. Leaders don't have to be feelers to be passionate about what they do.

Throughout Joshua's leadership career we catch glimpses of his passion. We see Joshua's passion when he confronted the heavenly visitor who was brandishing a sword. Without hesitation and with no contingent of soldiers backing him up, Joshua impulsively approached the messenger and demanded to know, "Are You for us or for our adversaries?" (Josh. 5:13).

When the ten spies returned from Canaan and began to terrify the Israelites with their accounts of giants, Scripture says, "But Joshua the son of Nun and Caleb the son of Jephunneh . . . tore their clothes; and they spoke to all the congregation of the children of Israel, saying . . ." (Num. 14:6–7). That's passion! Joshua and Caleb knew what was at stake. This was a pivotal moment. Tearing one's clothes symbolized great grief and sorrow over what was being done. If the Israelites failed to trust God now, the consequences would be severe.

When the Lord withdrew His presence from Joshua's army during their attack on the city of Ai, Joshua's forces were defeated. In a feverish outburst, Joshua again tore his clothes (he must have kept a seamstress on retainer), put dust on his head, and fell to the ground. He implored God:

> Alas, Lord GOD, why have You brought this people over the Jordan at all—to deliver us into the hand of the Amorites, to destroy us? Oh, that we had been content, and dwelt on the other side of the Jordan! O Lord, what shall I say when Israel turns its back before its enemies? For the Canaanites and all the inhabitants of the land will hear it, and surround us, and cut off our name from the earth. Then what will You do for Your great name? (Joshua 7:7–9)

Joshua was passionate in failure as well as in success. He was never complacent with either.

PERSONAL RESPONSE

How are passions and emotions the same?

_____

_____

_____

Can passion ever be felt without an open display of emotion?

_____

_____

_____

What are you the most passionate about today regarding your organization?

_____

_____

_____

How do you sustain your passion?

_____

_____

_____

Joshua was passionate in failure as well as in success. He was never complacent with either.

To what extent do you display your passion?

_____

_____

_____

Another sign of Joshua's passion for his work was his habit of rising early to perform his most difficult tasks. Whether it was attempting to cross the Jordan River, re-attacking the city of Ai, or looking to uncover a traitor in his ranks, Joshua rose early to start his day (Josh. 6:12; 7:16; 8:10). One mark of passionate leaders is the way they begin the day. Those who awaken in anticipation of what God might do still have their passion. Those who reluctantly or grumpily begin the day may no longer expect God to intervene in their lives. To them it is just another day.

Joshua remained passionate to the end of his life. At the close of his tenure he left Israel with this entreaty: "And if it seems evil to you to serve the LORD, choose for yourselves this day whom you will serve . . . But as for me and my house, we will serve the LORD" (Josh. 24:15). The passion for knowing God and doing His will never subsided within Joshua.

Why is passion important? People who accomplish great things are those who care a great deal about what they are doing. An apathetic leader is a contradiction in terms. Whether pastors, CEOs, or school principals, the people we meet who are making a difference in their worlds are passionate about their work.

Conversely, we meet pastors who tell us their churches are not growing and nothing good seems to be happening. Their monotone, impassionate demeanor hints that the stagnant conditions may originate in these pastors' attitudes.

Spiritual leaders are often those whose hearts are so tender they are never far from laughter or from tears. Whether in moments of epic triumph or inglorious defeat, great leaders are sensitive to the emotion of the moment. Their passion can be expressed either in celebration or sorrow almost simultaneously.

PERSONAL RESPONSE

How might you seek to become more sensitive to the passions of others?

_____

_____

_____

We have met leaders of small inner-city churches and fledgling Christian organizations, and heard them enthusiastically tell of the marvelous things God was

UNIT 9—JOSHUA'S LEADERSHIP PRINCIPLES

doing. Their ardor for what they sensed God was going to do through them inspired us to want to drop what we were doing and join with them. Such was the contagious nature of their zeal for God and His activity in their lives. Passion is not something you drum up within yourself. Either you have it or you don't. If you have lost it, it is imperative that you rediscover it.

A spiritual leader's passion comes from God. Spiritual leaders should be excited about what God is doing in their lives and exuberant about the possibilities of how God can impact others through them. Passion for God and His work gives leaders hope, even when circumstances appear grim.

God once made a promise to His people through His prophet Ezekiel: "I will give you a new heart and put a new spirit within you; I will take the heart of stone out of your flesh and give you a heart of flesh. I will put my Spirit within you" (Ezek. 36:26–27). Some of today's leaders desperately need God to do that for them. Over the years, their hearts have calcified under a steady stream of disappointments, criticisms, and failures. They have grown weary in well doing and have lost the heart to lead (Gal. 6:9). They still retain their leadership positions, but they retired from leading long ago.

Passion is not something you drum up within yourself. Either you have it or you don't.

PERSONAL RESPONSE

Have you lost a part of the passion you once felt for the goals God seemed to set before you? _____ Why did this happen? _____ How could you regain your passion for God-given goals?

_____

_____

_____

_____

DAY FOUR

JOSHUA WAS DECISIVE

Effective leadership relies heavily on the decision-making ability of the leader. Joshua was directing a precarious mission and handling the logistics of an extensive invading force. He could not afford to delay or waffle on his decisions. Like any good leader, he learned to make important decisions in a timely manner.

PERSONAL RESPONSE

What are the foremost challenges you face in making important decisions in a timely manner?

_____

_____

_____

_____

Joshua showed no hesitancy when God came to him and officially appointed him as Israel's new leader. Joshua immediately ordered the entire army to break camp; he gave them three days to prepare to march (Josh. 1:11). When Joshua was forced to deal with treachery in his own camp, he quickly tackled it head-on (Josh. 7:10–26).

Joshua promptly took his mighty men of valor and set out on an all-night march, thirty-five kilometers uphill, after receiving a desperate appeal for help from his allies, the Gibeonites. His timely decision and the sudden movement caught his enemies by surprise and helped secure him the victory (Josh. 10:6–10).

The leaders of the tribes of Ephraim and Manasseh once approached Joshua with a complaint. They were populous tribes and believed they required more land than had been allotted to them (Josh. 17:14). Their request put Joshua in an awkward position. Appearing to show favoritism toward a tribe, regardless of its size, could have created resentment among the others.

To make matters worse, Ephraim was Joshua's tribe. If he gave them what they wanted, he could appear to be favoring his family, friends, and even himself. Joshua wisely offered to give them more land, but it would be hill country covered with forests and allegedly inhabited by giants (Josh. 17:15). None of the other tribes could begrudge such a gift!

When the tribal leaders complained of the hazards of occupying those lands, Joshua didn't budge. He had given them a fair and reasonable offer, and he would not bend to any pressure. By deciding quickly and fairly, Joshua averted what could have been an extremely divisive controversy.

Smart leaders know that time is a precious resource and they cannot afford to waste it by lingering over decisions that must be made immediately. In matters of war, a delayed decision can cost lives. Likewise, a careless decision can lead to great sorrow. It is important that good leaders remain diligent in their responsibilities and are always prepared to make timely decisions. Spiritual leaders should act immediately upon receiving a clear word from God. To hear from God and then delay responding is not prudence; it is disobedience.

CONCEPT REFLECTION

CONCEPT: To hear from God and then delay responding is not prudence; it is disobedience.

How does God help leaders recognize His perfect timing?

_____

_____

_____

JOSHUA TOOK TIME TO WORSHIP

No one could ever accuse Joshua of having an easy life! The accumulated weight of his demeaning beginnings as a slave, the nomadic years in the wilderness, and the arduous experience of leading the people into Canaan might have demoralized another leader. But Joshua's confidence in God never seemed to waver; he never lost sight of his hope for the future, because he never strayed away from his relationship with God. At the outset of his work, God apprised him of the secret to success:

> This Book of the Law shall not depart from your mouth, but you shall meditate in it day and night, that you may observe to do according to all that is written in it. For then you will make your way prosperous, and then you will have good success. (Joshua 1:8)

BIBLE CONTEMPLATION

> **JOSHUA 1:8**
> _"This Book of the Law shall not depart from your mouth, but you shall meditate in it day and night, that you may observe to do according to all that is written in it. For then you will make your way prosperous, and then you will have good success."_

What does the phrase "this Book of the Law" mean to you?

_____

_____

_____

What does it mean to "meditate in it day and night"?

_____

_____

_____

What does it mean to "observe to do according to all that is written in it"?

_____

_____

_____

In your own words, define a "prosperous" way:

_____

_____

_____

What does it mean to you personally to "have good success"?

_____

_____

_____

As a military general, Joshua was a very busy man. He could have made excuses for not studying God's Word. He could have concluded that meditation was for those with the time for it. He could have questioned the relevancy of the Scriptures to a military officer, yet Joshua realized his walk with God had to come first. Not only would it determine his military success, his relationship with God would define every other form of success he would experience.

In addition to keeping God's Word himself, Joshua expected his soldiers to do likewise. When Joshua prepared his soldiers to advance into enemy territory, he ordered: "Sanctify yourselves, for tomorrow the LORD will do wonders among you" (Josh. 3:5).

Even while the Canaanite armies were uniting and arming themselves to attack, Joshua took time to worship God and to renew his people's covenant with God (Josh. 8:30–35). Joshua understood that whatever else he might need to set aside in the urgency of the moment, time with God was still a priority.

A spiritual leader can never afford to neglect his walk with God. Everything he does as a leader hinges on his relationship with the Lord. Historically, great

His relationship with God would define every other form of success he would experience.

spiritual leaders seized all the time necessary to ensure their devotional lives would be rich and full. Many rose early in the morning to begin their day with God.

Beginning each day with significant time in God's presence is not the prerogative of only pastors and missionaries. We know many corporate executives who rise as early as four o'clock to allow for unhurried time with God. Busy leaders regularly schedule appointments with key personnel, board members, clients, or donors. These same leaders, if they are wise, will understand that time scheduled with God is the most important meeting on their calendar. Just as meeting with God sustained Joshua as an army commander, so communing with God will help people from all walks of life successfully meet the challenges of the day.

PERSONAL RESPONSE

How could you build into your busy daily schedule more unhurried time with God?

_____

_____

_____

_____

ANOTHER LEADER IN GOD'S WORD

JESUS: AN UNWAVERING ROUTINE IN PRAYER

Good leaders follow a routine in prayer that ensures their priorities are not overlooked and their personal wholeness is enhanced. Jesus is our supreme example in this. Even though He seemed to follow a different schedule from day to day, Jesus was governed by an unwavering routine. Scripture tells us that Jesus habitually prayed late at night and early in the morning (Luke 6:12; Mark 1:35). Leaders need to establish a prayer routine that fits their particular responsibilities, schedules, and health needs, but it is paramount for all spiritual leaders to schedule regular and frequent times alone with their heavenly Father.

What kind of day did Jesus experience between His morning and night-time prayers?

- Jesus was never caught off guard by a day's events.

- Jesus was never in a hurry.

- Jesus showed no signs of experiencing stress in His daily ministry.

- Jesus never appeared to be overwhelmed or behind schedule.

Throughout His ministry, Jesus conveyed a tremendous serenity, confidence, and unwavering sense of purpose.

What is God saying to you about your need to establish a set prayer routine?

_____

_____

_____

DAY FIVE

JOSHUA BLESSED HIS FOLLOWERS

Leadership is all about people. It is influencing people for the corporate as well as their individual good.

Giving encouragement comes more naturally to some than to others. It is well known that effective leaders are generally good at encouraging their followers, but we have seen that truly great leaders do more than encourage their people—they bless them.

Joshua led people to accomplish corporate goals, but he did more than that. Joshua didn't use people; he blessed them. After Joshua led the Israelite forces to conquer Canaan, he released the tribes of Reuben, Gad, and Manasseh to return to their homes east of the Jordan River. Scripture indicates that before they departed, "Joshua blessed them" (Josh. 22:6). Perhaps Moses had taught Joshua the blessing God had taught him: "The LORD bless you and keep you; the LORD make His face shine upon you, and be gracious to you; the LORD lift up His countenance upon you, and give you peace" (Num. 6:24–26).

After all Joshua had accomplished as a general, he might have waited for them to present *him* with a plaque of appreciation or at least give a speech or two in his honor. Instead, Joshua took that final opportunity to bless his followers. Joshua never manipulated people to achieve his goals; he sought what was best for the people.

It would not have been surprising if, after waiting forty years to finally lead, Joshua had prodded his troops forward posthaste to finish the job his predecessor failed to accomplish. But throughout Joshua's leadership, he demonstrated a genuine concern for the spiritual well-being of his followers (Josh. 3:5; 5:2–9; 8:30–35; 23:1–24:28). Right to the end of Joshua's life, he was urging his country-

❧❧❧❧❧❧❧❧❧❧❧❧❧

Joshua didn't use people; he blessed them.

❧❧❧❧❧❧❧❧❧❧❧❧❧

men to walk closely with God. Even when it made no difference to his leadership, Joshua continued to express his concern for the people.

PERSONAL RESPONSE

What is the difference between encouraging others and blessing them?

_____

_____

_____

Good leaders are master encouragers. But there is a difference between simply encouraging someone and blessing them. A *good* leader will encourage someone to become a better worker; a *great* leader will bless someone so they become a better person. When you motivate people to work harder or to strive for excellence, you are helping them to become better followers, but you are not necessarily enabling them to become better people.

Perhaps in their efforts to produce more, church workers spend less and less time at home and their families are neglected. Or employees in the business world try to please the boss by taking work home every night. They may be highly motivated to accomplish more in their jobs, but they will be failing at home where the cost is dear.

True spiritual leaders know how to bless people so that their lives are better for having worked with them. To bless people is to bring their names before God and to request God's best for them. The apostle Paul's prayers recorded in Scripture are wonderful blessings he asked God to accomplish in people's lives. In his letters he let people know specifically what he was asking God to do for them (Eph. 1:15–23; 3:14–21; Phil. 1:9–11; Col. 1:9–11).

Often as leaders ask God to bless their followers, God will move the leader to be a practical part of the blessing. This may mean occasionally nudging task-oriented staff to leave the office at the end of the day and go home to their families. Spiritual leaders may take time to enquire about their employees' families. Blessing people certainly involves praying regularly for them and maybe with them as they seek God's will for their lives. Leaders find ways to strengthen those in their organizations, and by extension to bless their families as well.

> **To bless people is to bring their names before God and to request God's best for them.**

CONCEPT REFLECTION

CONCEPT: To bless people is to bring their names before God and to request God's best for them.

Identify several of your key followers or staff associates. What are you praying specifically for each of them?

PERSONNEL	PRAYER REQUEST
_____	_____
_____	_____
_____	_____
_____	_____
_____	_____
_____	_____
_____	_____
_____	_____
_____	_____

Many company employees or church volunteers work hard and give their best. After some have made many sacrifices "for the cause," they have been given a small plaque and ushered out the door. The world is full of people who feel they have been used and spent for the benefit of others. They look at a CEO receiving accolades for the company's success or they watch their pastor taking credit for burgeoning church programs, and they realize their leaders have merely used them as steps to their own success.

However, if you serve under a leader who knows how to bless others as God commanded, you should view the experience as an honor. If you had not been under the watchful, benevolent care of the leader God provided, you might not have weathered some of life's storms; you might never have grown as you have.

One test of whether you are blessing your followers is to watch how people respond to you (and to God) after they no longer work for you. Do they still keep in contact with you? Do they still seek your advice and welcome your input? Or do you hear through the grapevine that they are speaking ill of you to others? When you bless people, they will be your friends long after they are no longer your followers. And, more important, they will be stronger Christians because of your influence. Many will go further in God's will because God honored your prayers. You will see what you prayed for lived out and experienced in their lives. When you bless emerging leaders, you bless the future.

❦❦❦❦❦❦❦❦❦❦❦❦

When you bless emerging leaders, you bless the future.

❦❦❦❦❦❦❦❦❦❦❦❦

UNIT 9—JOSHUA'S LEADERSHIP PRINCIPLES

PERSONAL RESPONSE

How do you believe your current followers will respond to you (and to God) after they are no longer under the direct influence of your leadership?

_____

_____

_____

CONCEPT REFLECTION

CONCEPT: When you bless emerging leaders, you bless the future.

How could you bless someone you perceive to be an emerging leader?

EMERGING LEADER	BLESSING
_____	_____
_____	_____
_____	_____
_____	_____
_____	_____
_____	_____
_____	_____

ADDED INSIGHT INTO SPIRITUAL LEADERSHIP

A SHEPHERD'S HEART

In many ways, a godly leader is a shepherd of people. What is it that a shepherd does?

A good shepherd leads the sheep—who follow in the shepherd's footsteps and heed the sound of the shepherd's voice. In like manner, a godly leader provides an example to those who follow. A godly leader continually communicates with those who follow to encourage them forward in the leader's footsteps as the leader moves toward God-given goals and plans. A godly leader does not prod followers from behind, pushing them to move ahead solely on their own strength and ability.

A good shepherd is concerned with the entire life of each sheep in his flock—morning, noon, and night. A godly leader doesn't care for those who follow just during 9–5 working hours. Rather, a godly leader is concerned about the whole life of each person who is a follower, and especially so when that follower's family experiences a crisis or a milestone event, such as a wedding or the birth of a child.

A good shepherd also is concerned with the entire flock. He knows when a sheep is missing or sick, and he goes after the one who is straying. In like manner, a godly leader knows enough about *all* of those who follow to know their hurts, their doubts, and their struggles.

In what practical ways might you become a better shepherd of those whom God has given you as a flock?

THE ACTIVITY OF GOD

There are certain leadership skills that anyone can practice and incorporate into their leadership style. Learning to delegate, to communicate clearly, and to affirm others are all leadership practices that can be cultivated. In this regard, it is helpful to study the lives of leaders like Joshua to see what they did that made them such effective leaders.

When it comes to the development of spiritual leaders, the most important element is the activity of God in a person's life. You cannot mimic that, and it is not something you can achieve through practice or study. It comes through submission.

As people yield their lives entirely to God, God exercises His lordship over them and develops them into the leaders He wants them to be. God works in people's lives for *His* glory, not theirs. As we have seen, many people who are not practicing Christians exhibit good leadership traits. But Christians who allow God to mold their lives experience a dimension of spiritual leadership not possible in the secular realm. Their lives are used to dramatically impact the kingdom of God.

Spiritual leaders would do well to examine Joshua's leadership skills and to measure their own lives against his example. Then, in those areas where they fall short, they should humbly go before the Lord and ask Him to work those missing leadership traits into their lives. If God could take an ordinary man like Joshua and build into him the skills and character of a mighty spiritual leader, could He not do the same in your life?

God works in people's lives for *His* glory, not theirs.

JOSHUA: A PLACE IN HISTORY

The world was never the same after God touched Joshua's life. God took a man of no worldly consequence and made him into someone history cannot ignore. Joshua did not have extraordinary intelligence, unusual physical strength, or a remarkable appearance—nothing set him apart as destined for any degree of success. In fact, he was decidedly ordinary. What does stand out about him is his willingness to allow God to work so thoroughly in and through his life. God had total access to Joshua's life. Joshua's generation reaped the benefits, and we are still experiencing the results thousands of years later.

Before time, God intended to free a people from their bondage. Further, He planned to establish a special holy nation that would spiritually illuminate the rest of the world. To that kingdom of priests, God would send His only Son as the Savior for every person who would trust in Him. All this was in God's mind and heart before the land of Canaan was even formed. When the time came to put His plan into motion, God sought those He would use as leaders. First God used the patriarchs Abraham, Isaac, and Jacob. Four hundred years later, God called Moses. After Moses led the people as far as God would allow, God called Joshua.

Had Joshua lived a century earlier, we would probably never have heard of him. But in God's providence, Joshua was born at a critical moment in history. Every person's life intersects history—only a few impact it. How Joshua chose to respond to God would determine whether God used him in His plan. Joshua had a tender heart toward God. If God was looking for an instrument, Joshua was eager to be taken into his Master's hand. Joshua's availability to God led him to experience the profound joy of influencing his world and blessing God's people.

God did not simply transform Joshua into a godly individual. He fashioned him into a spiritual leader. Leaders don't live for themselves; they live for others. Their lives raise everyone around them to heights they would not otherwise achieve.

Leaders move people from where they are to where they must be. Spiritual leaders take people from where they are to the place God intends for them. Joshua did that.

Every person's life intersects history— only a few impact it.

Spiritual leaders take people from where they are to the place God intends for them.

ADDED INSIGHT INTO
SPIRITUAL LEADERSHIP

FIVE ONGOING ASPECTS OF INFLUENCE

There are five things that every good spiritual leader does in an ongoing way, day to day and year to year. These ongoing behaviors directly impact the influence the leader has:

1. Pray for the people in the organization, as well as those who might be served by the people in the organization (for example, customers).

2. Work hard; set a standard for going the extra mile.

3. Serve others with a heart of love; show genuine care for people as the Holy Spirit directs.

4. Maintain a positive, hopeful, faith-filled attitude; good morale in an organization is directly related to a leader's confidence and optimism

5. Communicate as fully and effectively as possible.

As you have read through the five ongoing behaviors directly associated with a leader's influence, has one or more of them stood out to you in a special way? What might you do to improve your behavior in this area?

_____

_____

_____

Every generation waits to see who is willing to be its spiritual leaders. God's plan from eternity includes our age. Surely God intends to do a great work and liberate people in this day. There are multitudes of people who need someone to help move them from where they are to the place God has for them.

But there is a price to be paid in becoming a spiritual leader; otherwise, there would be many more. Many Christians are satisfied with merely living out their individual existences, pursuing temporal pleasures, enjoying life to its fullest, and then departing this life to reside with God for eternity. Some are seduced into attempting to impact the world for their own gain or their own fame.

Deep within the hearts of others, however, is a sincere desire to live in a manner that makes a difference. These men and women want to leave the world a better place than when they first came into it. They know, as Joshua did, that they can do nothing of lasting significance apart from God. So they yield their lives to God and humbly ask Him to do whatever He must do to make them suitable instruments in His hands. A humble, committed, passionate servant of God is a perfect conduit for God to release His unparalleled power.

A humble, committed, passionate servant of God is a perfect conduit for God to release His unparalleled power.

Added Insight into Spiritual Leadership

The Pursuit of Excellence

Leaders need to be careful about how they use the word *excellence*. If *excellence* means "perfection," that is not God's standard. God's standard is doing things in a way that honors God. Excellence is generally applied to the doing of tasks, but a spiritual leader needs to be primarily concerned with *people*, not tasks. Organizations that concentrate more on tasks than on people miss what God considers most important. People are fallible and fickle. They can never produce perfection. When people are the focus of a leader's concern, the matter of excellence becomes a matter of giving God the best possible.

What is *your* understanding of excellence?

_____

_____

_____

How do you evaluate excellence within your organization?

_____

_____

_____

Drawing Some Personal Conclusions about Leadership

As you reflect back over your study of the life and leadership qualities of Joshua—and the ways in which God shaped Joshua to be the leader he became, take some time to review your thoughts about what it means to be a godly leader. In answering the questions below, you may want to review previous units in this workbook, including your personal responses to the Bible Contemplation, Personal Response, and Concept Reflection questions.

DAY ONE

1. Identify the best leader you've ever followed or were in a position to follow:

   _____

   What is the foremost lesson you learned from that person?

   _____

   _____

   _____

   _____

   What inspiration did you draw from this person for your own life? (UNIT 1)

   _____

   _____

   _____

   _____

2. Identify the worst leader you've ever followed or been in a position to follow:

   _____

   What is the foremost lesson you learned from that person?

   _____

   _____

   _____

   _____

   In what ways did consequences associated with this leader stand out as a graphic warning to you? (UNIT 1)

   _____

   _____

   _____

   _____

3. How has the way you began your relationship with God affected the way you walk with Him today? (UNIT 2)

_____

_____

_____

_____

4. What areas of your character have been the most affected since you began following Christ?

_____

_____

_____

_____

_____

Which areas is God presently working on?

_____

_____

_____

_____

How are you cooperating with God as He fashions your character? (UNIT 2)

_____

_____

_____

_____

5. Do you sense that God has a purpose for your life? If so, how would you describe that in one or two sentences? (UNIT 2)

_____

_____

_____

_____

6. How do you think God views your worship of Him?

_____

_____

_____

_____

When was the last time you had a life-changing encounter with God?

_____

_____

_____

_____

How could you deepen your walk with God? (UNIT 2)

_____

_____

_____

_____

7. What importance do you place on leading a life of faithfulness—and why so? (UNIT 2)

_____

_____

_____

_____

DAY TWO

1. Would you want someone to serve under you in the same manner you work under your leader? Why or why not? (UNIT 3)

_____

_____

_____

_____

2. What characteristics you have demonstrated as a follower indicate you could be a good leader? (UNIT 3)

_____

_____

_____

_____

_____

3. How does the history of your walk with God help you face today's challenges?

_____

_____

_____

_____

Do you resent the circumstances in your life right now?

_____

_____

_____

_____

What might God be seeking to teach you through them? (UNIT 3)

_____

_____

_____

_____

4. Do you value your relationship with God more highly than your position with people? What is the evidence? (UNIT 3)

_____

_____

_____

_____

_____

5. What do you do when you experience a time of spiritual barrenness? (UNIT 4)

_____

_____

_____

_____

6. Is God affirming you in your present leadership role? If so, what is the evidence God is pleased with your current leadership performance? (UNIT 4)

_____

_____

_____

_____

7. In what practical ways do you manifest reliance upon the Spirit of wisdom as you undertake your leadership responsibilities? (UNIT 4)

_____

_____

_____

_____

8. How often do you meditate on God's Word? How could you incorporate more time for meditation in your life? (UNIT 4)

_____

_____

_____

_____

9. Do you recognize God's voice? What have you heard Him say lately? (UNIT 4)

_____

_____

_____

_____

DAY THREE

1. Are you presently struggling under a difficult assignment? What is something God might want to teach you? (UNIT 5)

_____

_____

_____

_____

_____

2. How are you currently suffering the consequences of your past disobedience to God? What do you believe God desires for you to do? (UNIT 5)

_____

_____

_____

_____

_____

_____

_____

_____

3. What does your resistance to God's will indicate about human pride, and specifically about your own pride?

_____

_____

_____

What does it indicate about your relationship with Him? (UNIT 5)

_____

_____

_____

_____

4. What are the key events in your life that you believe have been most instru-
mental in shaping you into the person you are? (UNIT 6)

_____

_____

_____

_____

_____

5. What aspects of your character do you feel are displeasing to God?

_____

_____

_____

_____

What is God doing in you to change your character?

_____

_____

_____

_____

What are *you* doing? (UNIT 6)

_____

_____

_____

_____

6. Do other people believe that you have taken undo credit for your leadership
success? _____ How might you change that perception held by
others? (UNIT 6)

_____

_____

_____

_____

7. Do people with whom you work believe you care about them? _____
   How might you improve in caring for others? (UNIT 6)

   _____

   _____

   _____

   _____

8. Do you often consider the fact that one day you will give a full accounting
   to God for how you led others? _____ What do you anticipate
   that accounting will be like? (UNIT 6)

   _____

   _____

   _____

   _____

DAY FOUR

1. What do you sense God has promised to you in your future?

   _____

   _____

   _____

   _____

2. Is God presently asking you to trust Him for a specific promise?_____
   What challenges are you experiencing as you trust Him one step at a time?
   (UNIT 7)

   _____

   _____

   _____

   _____

   Does the way you are living your life reflect a confidence that God will do
   what He promised? (UNIT 7) _____

3. Are you presently struggling to move your followers forward? If so, why do you believe your followers are failing to move as you desire?

_____

_____

_____

_____

Could the failure have anything to do with your lack of accessibility, confidence, or optimism? (UNIT 8) _____

4. Do the people with whom you work trust you? Should they? (UNIT 8)

_____

5. What positive events or attitudes in your home reflect your leadership? (UNIT 8)

_____

_____

_____

_____

_____

6. Is there any evidence you have influence with God? (UNIT 8) _____

7. How is your life impacting the future? (UNIT 8)

_____

_____

_____

_____

8. Are you helping your coworkers draw closer to God? Be specific in your answer. (UNIT 8)

_____

_____

_____

_____

DAY FIVE

1. Do you consider yourself to be an effective leader? Why, or why not? (UNIT 9)

_____

_____

_____

_____

_____

2. What is God presently doing in your life to make you a better leader? (UNIT 9)

_____

_____

_____

_____

3. Are you relentlessly pursuing your organization's God-given mission? If not, why not? If so, in what ways?

_____

_____

_____

_____

How might you do more as a leader? (UNIT 9)

_____

_____

_____

_____

4. In what ways are you a blessing to those you work with?

_____

_____

_____

_____

How are people better for having worked with you? (UNIT 9)

_____

_____

_____

_____

5. In what ways can you see that God placed you precisely in the position you are in, at the time you are in it? (UNIT 10)

_____

_____

_____

_____

6. Of all the leadership principles and concepts covered in this book, which three principles or concepts stand out as being the most important to you personally at this present time? (UNIT 10)

_____

_____

_____

ABOUT THE AUTHORS

HENRY BLACKABY and his wife, Marilynn, have five children, all of whom are actively serving in full-time Christian ministry. They also have fourteen grandchildren. Dr. Blackaby graduated from the University of British Columbia and Golden Gate Baptist Theological Seminary. He has also been granted four honorary doctoral degrees. He has authored numerous books, many with his children. His best-known work is *Experiencing God: Knowing and Doing the Will of God*. He previously coauthored eight books with his son Richard, including *Experiencing God: Day by Day; Spiritual Leadership: Moving People on to God's Agenda;* and *Hearing God's Voice*. Dr. Blackaby speaks worldwide and regularly consults with Christian CEOs in America on issues related to spiritual leadership.

RICHARD BLACKABY is the oldest son of Henry and Marilynn. He previously coauthored eight books with his father, including, *Experiencing God: Day by Day; Spiritual Leadership;* and *Hearing God's Voice*. He is married to Lisa and has three teenage children, Mike, Daniel, and Carrie. Richard was the pastor of Friendship Baptist Church, Winnipeg, before becoming the president of the Canadian Southern Baptist Seminary in Cochrane, Alberta, Canada. He travels widely, speaking on the subject of spiritual leadership.

For more information contact:

Blackaby Ministries International

P.O. Box 161228

Atlanta, GA 30321

404.362.9500

404.362.9825

information@blackaby.org

www.blackaby.org

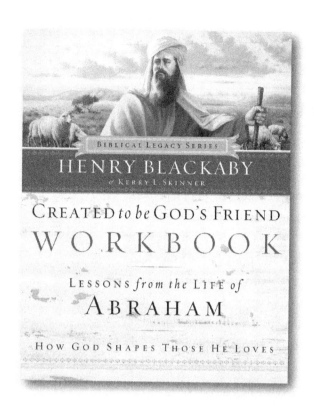

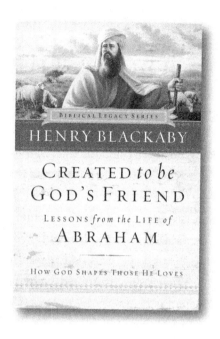

From the example of the life of Abraham,
Henry Blackaby will show you how to become God's intimate friend.
In this the first book in the Biblical Legacy Series, you will learn how God shapes those He loves into
useful, joyful co-workers as they hear and respond to His call in everyday life.
Created to Be God's Friend is a remarkable study of our relationship with a personal God
who is constantly working in each of our lives.

Book ISBN: 0-7852-6982-7

Workbook ISBN: 0-7852-6758-1

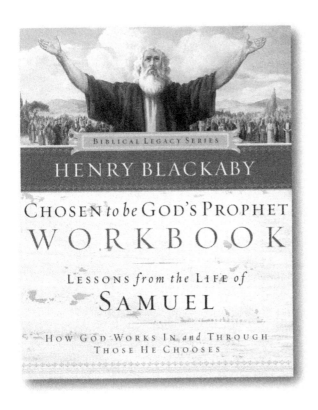
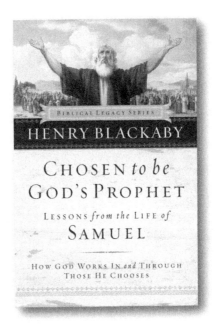

Samuel's life was full of incredible—and defining—moments as God shaped him and guided him.
As readers observe how God moved in Samuel's life, they will recognize those moments in their own
lives; moments that are so different from the run-of-the-mill ones.
God uses these "divine moments," which often come during times of crisis,
to bring His purposes to pass.

By taking a glimpse into what God did in Samuel's life,
Dr. Blackaby enables readers to define those critical times in their lives
when God selects us as His chosen servants.
Chosen to Be God's Prophet is the second selection in the Biblical Legacy Series
offered by Thomas Nelson Publishers.

Book ISBN: 0-7852-6555-4

Workbook ISBN: 0-7852-6557-0

CPSIA information can be obtained at www.ICGtesting.com
Printed in the USA
LVOW02s2153011015

456566LV00001B/1/P